Fife Pilgrim Way

Duncan Weaver and Jacquetta Megarry

Rucksack Readers

Fife Pilgrim Way

First published 2024 by Rucksack Readers,
6 Old Church Lane, Edinburgh, EH15 3PX, UK

Phone   0131 661 0262 (+44 131 661 0262)
Email: *info@rucsacs.com*
Website   *www.rucsacs.com*

Text, design and mapping are copyright Rucksack Readers © 2024; photos are copyright Rucksack Readers and licensors: see page 71 for credits.

The right of Duncan Weaver and Jacquetta Megarry to be identified as the authors of this work has been asserted by them in accordance with the Copyright, Designs and Patents Act 1988.

All rights reserved. No part of this publication may be reproduced, stored in a retrieval system, or transmitted in any form or by any means, electronic, mechanical, photocopying, recording or otherwise, without prior permission in writing from the publisher and copyright holders.

ISBN 978-1-913817-18-3

British Library cataloguing in publication data: a catalogue record for this book is available from the British Library.

Design and illustrations by Ian Clydesdale: *ian@clydesdale.scot*

Printed on rainproof, biodegradable paper in the Czech Republic via Akcent Media of St Neots, UK

The mapping in this book is © Rucksack Readers, commissioned from Lovell Johns Ltd: *www.lovelljohns.com*. The mapping contains Ordnance Survey data © Crown copyright and database right 2023-24.

Publisher's note

All information was checked carefully prior to publication. However, new services start up, rural businesses open and close, and routes evolve. Along the route, look out for waymarkers and follow any local diversions. Prior to departure, please check: *bit.ly/RR-FPW*

The weather in Scotland is unpredictable year-round, and parts of the Way are exposed and remote from sources of help. Do not rely on having reception on a mobile phone. You are responsible for your own safety, and for ensuring that your clothing, food and equipment are suited to your needs. The publisher cannot accept any liability for any ill-health, accident or loss arising directly or indirectly from reading this book.

Feedback is welcome and will be rewarded

We welcome comments and suggestions: please email us at **info@rucsacs.com**. All feedback will be followed up, and if comments lead to changes, readers will be entitled to claim a free copy of our next edition upon publication.

Contents

	Foreword	4
1	**Planning to walk the Way**	
	Best time of year and weather	5
	How long will it take?	6
	Cycling the Way	6
	Which direction?	7
	Experience, safety and road walking	7
	Accommodation and refreshments	8
	Getting there and away	9
	Terrain and gradients	10
	Scottish Outdoor Access Code and animals	11
	Waymarking and navigation	12
	Local names of features	13
	Packing checklist	13
2	**Background information**	
	2·1 Fife: a pilgrim kingdom	14
	2·2 Miners and mining	20
	2·3 Habitats and wildlife	24
3	**Route description**	
	Culross	28
	3·1a Culross to Dunfermline	29
	3·1b North Queensferry to Dunfermline	34
	Dunfermline	41
	3·2 Dunfermline to Crosshill	42
	3·3 Crosshill to Leslie	48
	Glenrothes	51
	3·4 Leslie to Kennoway	52
	3·5 Kennoway to Ceres	57
	3·6 Ceres to St Andrews	63
	St Andrews	68
4	**Reference**	
	Organisations, accommodation, maps and further reading	70
	Weather, notes for novices and transport	71
	Acknowledgements, credits and churches along the Way	71
	Index	72

Foreword

I am really delighted to recommend this guide to walking or cycling the Fife Pilgrim Way. Like its companion guidebooks, it is well-planned, concise, clear and beautifully illustrated. Fife is an ancient Pictish kingdom that became an earldom. It is compact, with a picturesque identity of its own, as well as being reasonably flat and therefore walkable and cyclable.

The historic places of pilgrimage are Dunfermline, where the remains of St Margaret were originally buried, and St Andrews, with its great cathedral which at one time held relics of the disciple of Jesus. As ever, there are subsidiary sites of pilgrimage and other saints to remember. Dunfermline is also the burial place of Robert the Bruce, Scotland's great warrior king.

St Andrews, as the site of Scotland's oldest university, was a key location in the Scottish Reformation. It was here that the young Patrick Hamilton, Scotland's first Protestant martyr, was burned to death in 1528. The stake was set up outside St Salvator's College, at a spot marked today by the letters PH set into the cobbles. Students still consider it unlucky to tread on his initials.

Hamiilton's execution was slow and horrific. A witness recorded that he was more roasted than burned – *ustulatus magis quam combustus*. John Knox recorded how the gunpowder used as a firelighter scorched Hamilton, but failed to set the wood alight and a baker called Myrtoun ran off to bring an armful of straw. Patrick Hamilton suffered for some six hours. There can be few places in Scotland so evocative of martyrdom.

The route winds through the heartlands of Fife, passing the heritage of its coal mining industry – now long exhausted, but once a source of great wealth. Lochore coalfield formerly supported seven mines, but has been transformed into the splendid recreational resource that is Lochore Meadows Country Park: see page 22. And where there were miners, there was beer. The route passes three historic Gothenburg public houses, set up on a Swedish model and devoting their profits to communal facilities; their locations are given on page 23. They may prove a blessing for the pilgrims of today.

Welcome to a thought-provoking pilgrimage through Fife's religious history, industrial heritage and inspiring scenery.

Professor Sir Iain Torrance KCVO
Former Dean of the Chapel Royal in Scotland and Dean of the Thistle

1 Planning to walk the Way

The Fife Pilgrim Way follows the ancient medieval pilgrim route which ran across the Kingdom of Fife to the cathedral of St Andrews. This route was recreated in 2019 with the unusual feature of a choice of starting points – Culross or North Queensferry – and a total of 65 miles of waymarked trail. Both places are important in the history of pilgrimage in Fife. Culross is a picturesque conservation village, and at the top of its steep hill you can visit the remains of its 13th century Cistercian Abbey. Its ecclesiastical roots go back much further to two saints – St Serf and St Mungo (Kentigern).

North Queensferry is so named because of St Margaret (1045-1093) who established a regular ferry at this crossing of the Forth, which she made free for pilgrims. This was probably some time after she became Queen of Scotland in 1070. The two branches of the route converge after 8·5 miles (14 km) at Dunfermline Abbey, the successor to the Benedictine abbey which Margaret had founded in 1072. The route then winds for a further 47 miles (76 km) across the heartlands of Fife to finish at the ruins of St Andrews Cathedral.

Best time of year and weather

The Way does not take you through exposed or isolated terrain, so in theory you could complete it at any time of year. However hours of daylight in Scotland are short between November and January, many facilities close out of season, and the weather is apt to be wet and windy. Realistically, it is better to set out between early May and mid October. The countryside and wildlife are more vibrant in spring; from late March onwards there is more than 12 hours of daylight and after Easter more facilities are open; in September/October autumn colour in the foliage may be an added attraction, and everywhere is less busy than July/August.

At any time of year, the weather in Scotland is unpredictable, although short-range forecasts are reliable. Statistically, the best months are May and September – but periods of good or bad weather can occur at any time of year. The route is usable in all weathers: the important thing is to be well prepared. Always carry reliable waterproofs, in summer use sun protection and check the forecast before you set out: see page 71.

The Way through Lochore Meadows Country Park

How long will it take?

The Way runs mainly on good footpaths with a few short climbs and descents, so it offers long-distance walking that is generally relatively easy. During and after wet weather, especially in winter months, some sections can become very muddy. Although the distance can be divided up in many ways, in this book we have divided it into seven sections (of which, with a choice of starting section, you will walk six) with an average length of only 9·3 miles/15 km each: see Table 1. This is to ensure that each section finishes at a place where there are some facilities, and public transport that allows you to reach a wider selection. It also allows time for walking offroute and travel time at the start and end of each section if need be.

How many days you will spend depends on the size of your group (larger groups travel at or below the speed of the slowest member) as well as your speed of walking. How often you stop for photos, rests and side-trips is a major factor. On a pilgrimage route you may wish time to contemplate and reflect, and having an excessive daily distance to cover may spoil your enjoyment of the route. On the other hand, if you are a fit, experienced long-distance walker, you may wish to combine a couple of sections. As we finalise for press in 2024, there is no accommodation on or very close to the route between Dunfermline and Glenrothes, so if you regard 18 miles as a feasible day walk then you might yomp it without an overnight break.

When planning your itinerary, be aware that there is a general shortage of accommodation in certain places; you may have to use transport to reach a suitable place to stay. If you have very limited time, you could use public transport to skip a section or two, or consider cycling some sections: see below.

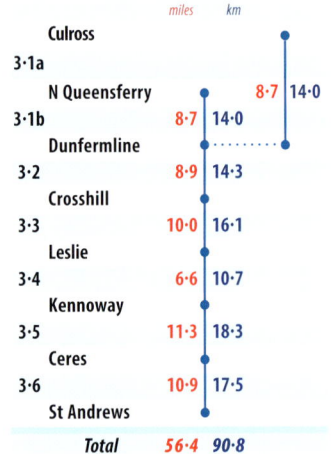

Table 1 Distances for the Way

Section	Place	miles	km
	Culross		
3·1a		8·7	14·0
	N Queensferry		
3·1b		8·7	14·0
	Dunfermline		
3·2		8·9	14·3
	Crosshill		
3·3		10·0	16·1
	Leslie		
3·4		6·6	10·7
	Kennoway		
3·5		11·3	18·3
	Ceres		
3·6		10·9	17·5
	St Andrews		
	Total	**56·4**	**90·8**

Cycling the Way

It is possible to cycle the Way on a bike with suitable tyres and gears: we recommend a gravel or mountain bike. There are places where you will have to dismount to go through gates, but there are no stiles on the Way. There are quite a few stretches where you would probably have to push your bike along a field-edge path, though this may also depend on how fat the tyres and how soft the ground. During and after wet weather there may be several stretches muddy enough that you need to dismount so as to fulfil the SOAC requirement for responsible cycling: see page 70.

Whilst it is possible for a fit and experienced cyclist to complete the route in a day, you need at least two days to truly enjoy the Way and its surroundings. You could also combine cycling some sections with walking others. There are four bike shops along the route – in Dunfermline, Leslie, Glenrothes and St Andrews.

Which direction?

Although you could follow the route from east to west, this guidebook is written on the assumption that, like a medieval pilgrim, you will finish at St Andrews Cathedral. There is also a practical reason to follow the route eastwards in that you are much more likely to have the wind behind you. Although the wind in Fife is not always from the south-west, when it blows strongly, with or without rain, it is almost invariably south-westerly.

Experience, safety and road walking

The Way is suitable for newcomers to long-distance walking, with its modest daily distances, excellent waymarking and good public transport connections. If you are a total beginner, and especially if planning to go alone, we recommend you obtain our *Notes for novices*: see page 71. The most important advice is never to underestimate the number of hours that you need to cover the distance, especially if aiming for a public transport connection at the end of the day's walk. There is little merit in undertaking a pilgrimage under time-pressure or as a test of endurance.

Walking in Fife should be a safe and enjoyable activity, but it's always prudent to ensure that your waterproofs are fit for purpose and to check the short-range weather forecast to find out whether they will be needed: see page 71. Carry enough drinking water and snacks to last between supply points and wear clothing in layers so as to manage your body temperature.

Although much of the route runs on footpaths and on farm or forest tracks, there are some sections on roads, mostly with pavements. Where there's no pavement or verge, always walk on the right so as to face oncoming traffic. Be mindful of sight lines: when approaching a blind bend to the right it's often better to veer away from the road edge so as to see and be seen. If walking in twilight, be sure to wear bright colours or reflective bands.

Accommodation and refreshments

	B&B/hotel	hostel/bunkhouse	café/pub	shop	campsite
Culross	✓		✓		
Cairneyhill	✓			✓	
Crossford	✓		✓	✓	
N Queensferry	✓		✓		
Rosyth	✓				
Dunfermline	✓		✓	✓	
Kelty			✓	✓	
Crosshill			✓	✓	
Lochore			✓		
Capledrae Farm 0·9 miles offroute		✓			
Kinglassie			✓	✓	
Leslie			✓	✓	
Glenrothes	✓		✓	✓	
Markinch	✓		✓	✓	✓
Windygates			✓		
Kennoway			✓	✓	
Chance Inn 1·6 miles offroute			✓		✓
Ceres	✓		✓	✓	
Pitscottie			✓		
Craigtoun			✓		✓
St Andrews	✓	✓	✓	✓	✓

Fife has long been a popular holiday destination with plenty of accommodation such as hotels, B&Bs, self-catering cottages and campsites. To unsupported walkers, accommodation is only attractive if it is on or very close to the route. Sadly, at present such options are very limited, and budget options are even harder to find.

Camping is the ultimate low-cost, self-reliant option: carry a tent for utmost flexibility. However it requires some planning, and we know of only four campsites that accept one-night tents anywhere near the route, none of them west of Markinch. All are shown on the mapping and listed in the table above. Although wild camping is allowed in Scotland if it is done responsibly (see the Scottish Outdoor Access Code, page 11), much of the Way passes through urban areas and farmland with few if any suitable sites.

One approach is to stay in one place for several nights and use transport, either public or private, to reach the start and to return from the finish of each section. Sometimes you can resolve the logistics by walking the sections out of order, or by getting help from your accommodation provider.

Stagecoach runs buses throughout Fife and all sections start and end on one of their bus routes. Moffat and Williamson also run buses in and around St Andrews: ***www.moffat-williamson.co.uk***. Many local churches along the Way are keen to support walkers along the FPW and if contacted may be willing to offer shelter and basic facilities inside their buildings. See the list of churches on page 71.

There are cafés and shops at the beginning and end of each section, but in between such facilities are sparse or non-existent. Therefore, go prepared with all the drinking water and food that you need for the day. This is specially important if you have any dietary restrictions or allergies.

Getting there and away

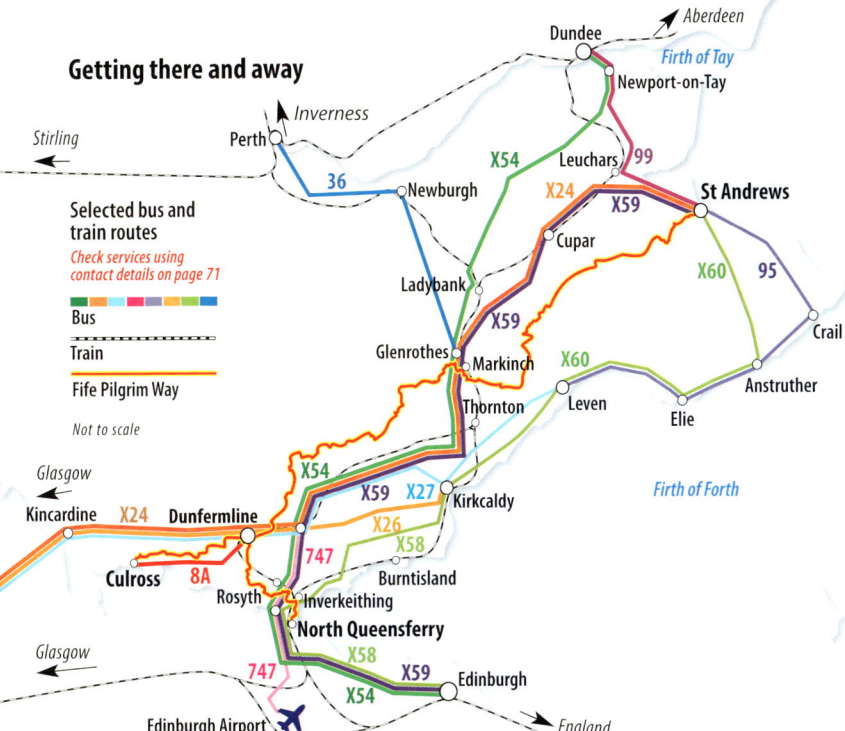

Selected bus and train routes
Check services using contact details on page 71
Bus
Train
Fife Pilgrim Way

Not to scale

Glasgow and Edinburgh airports have a wide range of international flights. From Edinburgh airport, take Stagecoach bus 747 to Ferrytoll and once over the bridge, alight and go down the steps into North Queensferry. (Bus 747 also reaches Inverkeithing with a journey time of 30 minutes.). To reach Culross instead, take the train or bus to Dunfermline (on some bus routes you have to change at Rosyth) and then bus 8A to Culross as below.

From Glasgow airport, you need to reach Glasgow Queen Street station (not Glasgow Central) and take a train to Edinburgh Haymarket. From there, take the train or bus to Dunfermline and then bus 8A to Culross as below. Note that the Dunfermline bus station is about 0·7 miles (1·1 km) from its City Station: see the town plan on page 41.

Starting from central Edinburgh, it takes about 20 minutes by train from Waverley (a few minutes less from Haymarket) direct to North Queensferry station to begin the Way there. Stagecoach buses take a little longer (30 minutes) but are more frequent (every 15 minutes), from Edinburgh's bus station. To start from Culross instead, you first need to reach Dunfermline by train or bus, then take a Stagecoach bus 8A to Culross.

To return from St Andrews, one option is the frequent Stagecoach 99 bus to Leuchars to join the rail network, journey time 11 minutes. Alternatively take a 22-minute bus to Cupar (X24 or X59) and then an onward train. Or use the hourly X59 service direct to Edinburgh, with a journey time of just over two hours. Bus numbers followed by an X means it's an express service in a vehicle that's more like a coach – quieter and more comfortable than the smaller buses.

Terrain and gradients

The route runs along a mixture of footpaths, tracks, unsurfaced roads and tarmac when on minor roads and pavements. The route is generally low-level, rising only to 230 m/755 ft near the top of Clatto Hill – its highest point. There are no extensive or especially steep climbs or descents, so the route is accessible to any healthy walker: see the altitude profile below.

Your decision on footwear depends on your approach: if walking the entire route in normal Scottish weather (mixed), you probably need waterproof walking boots. In dry conditions, you may find that trainers or walking shoes with good grippy soles will suffice, especially if you combine them with ankle gaiters to help keep out rain and squelchy mud. If walking the Way in sections, your footwear can vary from day to day, whereas through walkers need footwear to suit the worst conditions they may encounter. If you can take only one piece of footwear, we advise walking boots unless you are extremely confident of dry ground and dry weather.

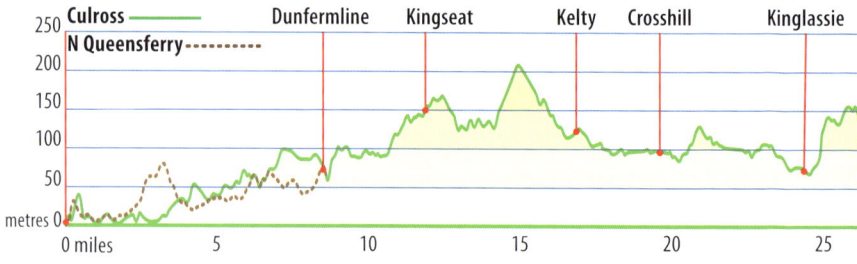

The Scottish Outdoor Access Code and animals

Enjoy Scotland's outdoors responsibly

KNOW THE CODE BEFORE YOU GO
outdooraccess-scotland.scot

Everyone has the right to be on most land and inland water providing they act responsibly. Your access rights and responsibilities are explained fully in the Scottish Outdoor Access Code.

Whether you're in the outdoors or managing the outdoors, the key things are to:

- **take responsibility for your own actions**
- **respect the interests of other people**
- **care for the environment.**

Visit **outdooraccess-scotland.scot** for full details.

Under the SOAC, everyone has the statutory right to access to land for recreational purposes. Access rights must be exercised responsibly. They apply to most land in Scotland, including that which is privately owned, with the exceptions of gardens, farmyards and cultivated crops. For a summary of the Code, see the panel above. For full details of the Code, including leaflets for dog owners and cyclists, please visit *www.outdooraccess-scotland.com*.

The route of the Fife Pilgrim Way has been negotiated with land managers and owners and it is important to respect their rights and maintain their goodwill. Keep to the signed path, especially around field edges, and take care to leave gates as you find them, open or shut.

Dog owners should think twice before taking their pets along. Dogs must be kept under close control at all times, with particular care when near livestock. Never allow your dog to approach sheep or cows that are, or may be, pregnant or with young. Coming between cattle and their young is dangerous, especially with a dog. You would also have to seek dog-friendly accommodation and would have very limited options for an evening meal.

The route runs adjacent to farmland with livestock in many places. It goes through several farmyards where cattle or sheep may be crossing the route: these are at Knockhouse Farm (mile 7, page 31), Clatto Farm (mile 41·7, page 58) and Kinninmonth Farm (mile 48·2, page 63). Take care around livestock, particularly when going through these farmyards.

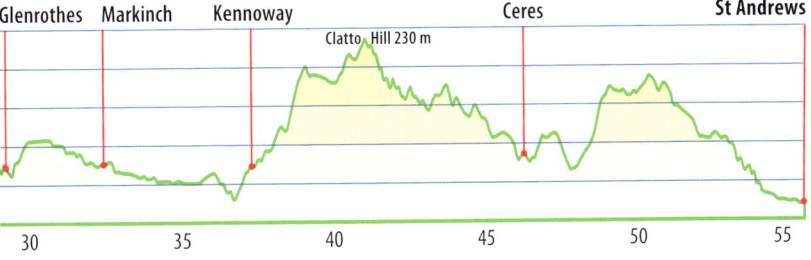

Waymarking and navigation

The route is well marked throughout, almost invariably with the distinctive FPW logo. The logo is based on a badge discovered in 1998 during excavations at St Andrews Castle. Medieval pilgrims may have received and treasured such badges upon completion. It shows the apostle Andrew being crucified on a diagonal cross. Above his head is a crown, symbolising the royal palace at Dunfermline, and beneath it is a version of the distinctive cross carved at the entrance to the tower of St Drostan's Church, Markinch. Opposite the two holes (used for stitching the badge), the border is incomplete, like that of the original discovery; it symbolises the unfinished nature of all our journeys on earth.

Look out for FPW signs that are displayed in a variety of different sizes and colours – as stickers attached to posts, as circular signs on gates and on their own dedicated poles. On occasion, you may need to follow a green fingerpost without any logo, as in the photo above. There are large signboards at intervals along the route, many decorated with stained glass: see the photos on pages 29, 33 and 34. Also look out for circular FPW metal plaques set into the pavement at various locations. There are no separate signs for cyclists, who may follow the same route as walkers, dismounting where necessary to push their bikes.

Although the signage is generally very good, inevitably in the long term waymarking suffers from the effects of weather, animals and humans. On occasion you may reach an unsigned junction: if so, refer to our instructions and mapping. If you carry a smartphone, you can refer to our online route map and/or the Ordnance Survey app OSMaps: for both, see page 70. Be aware that as of 2024 the OS route line is incorrect in several places which we list on page 70 so you won't be led astray.

Be aware also of the Fife Coastal Path which shares part of the FPW route near the beginning – whether you start from Culross or North Queensferry. Recognise its logo (a wavy green, yellow, blue, symbolising hills, beach and sea) and know when to follow it and when to ignore it.

Local names of features

A number of words crop up repeatedly in the names of features or streets that may not be familiar to readers from outside Scotland. Here are some examples:

brae	steep slope or hillside
burn	stream
craig	crags, rocky outcrop
den	narrow valley or ravine, often wooded
gate	road or roadway
glen	valley – broader than a den but not as flat as a strath
kirk	church
law	hill
loan	lane or narrow road, often rural
loch, lochan	lake, small lake
wynd	narrow lane or alley, often historic
yett	gate

Packing checklist

If you are tackling the whole route in a single exedition, you may need most or all of what we list below. Some items may be unnecessary if you are going with a good weather forecast. On day-trips, many items won't be needed, obviously.

Essential
- rucksack (e.g 25-35 litres)
- waterproof rucksack cover or liner(s)
- comfortable walking boots and/or shoes
- specialist walking socks
- waterproof jacket and overtrousers
- clothing in layers (tops, trousers, jacket)
- hats for warmth and sun protection
- gloves
- guidebook with maps
- water carrier and plenty of water
- food for the more remote sections
- first aid kit, including blister treatment
- toilet tissue (biodegradable)
- overnight kit including toiletries
- insect repellent, sun protection (summer)

Desirable
- walking poles
- spare socks
- gaiters
- plastic bag(s) for litter
- camera and spare memory card
- spare batteries or charger for camera
- binoculars (useful for wildlife)
- notebook and pen
- pouch or secure pockets for keeping small items handy and safe
- mobile phone and charger.

For campers
The above list assumes that you are using B&Bs. If you are camping, you'll also need a tent, sleeping gear, cooking utensils, portable stove, fuel and food, and a much larger rucksack to carry it all.

2·1 Fife: a pilgrim kingdom

Fife is known as the pilgrim kingdom because of two crucial places – Dunfermline and St Andrews. During medieval times, thousands would come from Britain and beyond to visit the shrines of two major saints – St Margaret at Dunfermline Abbey and that of the apostle St Andrew in its cathedral.

During medieval times, for many people, undertaking a pilgrimage was seen as building up credit in heaven or as part of a penance. Penitents walked with a sense of contrition in the hope that they might receive forgiveness by atoning for their sins. It could even be imposed by the courts, with a tariff of four major pilgrimages as a sentence for murder in the 15th century.

Veneration of saints and belief in the miraculous powers of their relics was at its height. Both people and priests believed that saints had the power to deal directly with God. Churches were festooned with statues, murals, and ornate rood screens, and people attributed miraculous powers to relics ranging from bones to items of clothing.

Thankfulness was another motivation. Pilgrims journeyed because they were grateful for overcoming an illness, the birth of a child or the blessing of a good harvest or prosperous business. Some saw pilgrimage as an opportunity to escape from their humdrum lives and experience the novelty and pleasure of a new landscape and people. Perhaps the medieval pilgrim had more in common with the modern tourist than we realise.

Pilgrim numbers had started to dwindle within Fife even before the rise of Protestantism in the 16th century and the banning of religious pilgrimage by the Scottish Parliament in 1581 However, the past 20 years has seen a remarkable revival of many former pilgrimage routes across Europe, especially in Protestant countries, in contrast with the decline in church attendance. The Scottish Pilgrim Routes Forum currently recognises eleven such routes at various stages of development: see **www.sprf.org.uk**.

The recovery of pilgrimage partly reflects a modern need to be surrounded by nature, taking time out from the pace and stress of modern life. Many are attracted to the spiritual element and the simplicity of a journey in which you merely put one foot after the next until you reach your destination. There is also joy when you discover new people and places, and can savour a sense of completion.

Culross Abbey

A choice of starting points

Along with the choice of starting points comes a choice of saints. If you opt for Culross, you are linking with the Celtic Christianity of the fifth to seventh centuries. Long before 1217 when the Cistercian abbey was founded in Culross by Malcolm, 7th Earl of Fife, this site above Culross was a Celtic Christian place of worship linked with St Serf and his pupil, St Mungo (aka Kentigern). The abbey was dedicated to St Mary and St Serf.

Centuries later, in about 1500, the Abbot had most of the nave demolished, following a trend of focusing inward on the monks rather than outward into the community. He also built an 84-foot tower at the choir's western end. After the Reformation in 1560, the monks' choir and tower were repurposed as a parish church, and legally recognised as such in 1633. A major renovation took place in 1824, and restoration under architect Robert Rowand Anderson followed in 1905.

After leaving Culross, you pass a ruined chapel dedicated to St Mungo: see page 30. It was founded in 1503 by the Archbishop of Glasgow and stands on the site where St Thenew is said to have given birth to St Mungo. It was excavated in 1926 and you see the full extent of its nave and chancel, with the altar intact at its eastern end – all at what seems a vulnerable roadside location.

The other starting point is from North Queensferry, firmly following the tradition of St Margaret. She was a Hungarian-born princess born about 1045, whose exiled father Edward was a potential heir to the English throne. After his death and the arrival of William the Conqueror, Margaret's family fled to Northumbria from where they tried to return to the continent.

Their ship was blown off course and in 1068 she arrived in Scotland as a refugee. King Malcolm III of Scotland offered her protection, and later marriage. Their wedding was at Dunfermline Palace in 1070, and Margaret became a strong influence.

Malcolm greets Margaret on arrival

They had eight children together, six sons and two daughters. Three of her sons and one stepson became King of Scotland, and her impact persisted for 60 years after her own death, until that of her youngest son King David I in 1153.

As a devout Christian, she used her status and wealth to build many churches throughout Scotland. She created the villages on the shores of the Forth to ensure regular ferries for pilgrims travelling to St Andrews. Margaret probably used the ferry crossing regularly to travel between the then capital of Dunfermline and Edinburgh Castle. It became known as the Queen's Ferry and the villages on either shore known as North and South Queensferry.

Margaret's head-shrine (replica)

Dunfermline

Either way, your first section ends at Dunfermline. Its ruined abbey and palace both feature in Margaret's story. Pilgrims began to visit and venerate her tomb soon after her death in 1093. By 1180 the pilgrim traffic justified moving it to near the high altar and placing an elaborate reliquary decorated with carvings and gold leaf to house her various relics. In 1250, the chapel at the eastern end of the abbey was built specifically for her enshrinement on 19 June.

The campaign to have her canonised had begun five years earlier, but at first Pope Innocent IV declined on the grounds that she was not credited with enough miracles. A list of 45 miracles was compiled, most of them dramatic healings of fevers, tumours, blindness and 'demonic possession' – often after the sufferer had spent all night alone in the abbey.

By 1249 or 1250, the Pope had relented and Queen Margaret became Saint Margaret. Candles burned constantly around her tomb, and relics were displayed in all their splendour, including a gilded head-shrine – of which the case could be raised to reveal part of her skull. Another was her night-dress, which became popular with Scottish queens to wear in late-stage pregnancy to promote successful labour. For the next three centuries, the pilgrim trade was brisk.

Then the Protestant Reformation arrived, and between September 1559 and June 1560 the 'cleansing' of the abbey was swift and brutal. The shrine was desecrated, the royal tombs and altars damaged and the monks left. The abbey itself fell into disrepair, roofless in places and with walls so weakened that they needed massive buttressing in the 1620s.

In early Victorian times, a new parish church was built on the site of the former choir. It still celebrates Margaret's role in several places, including the stained glass of the west window.

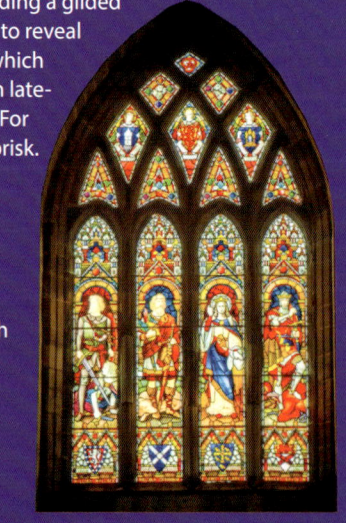
St Margaret, west window, Dunfermline Abbey

St Margaret's shrine and its precious relics had been lost or destroyed. All that now remains is its marble base made of fossilised seashells, outside the east end of the church. Her only surviving relic (allegedly a shoulder bone) is not here, but in St Margaret's Memorial Church, which the Way passes: see page 42. It was donated to the church in 2008 and housed in the altar of its Lady Chapel. In the porch area, the replica of Margaret's head-shrine is on display. The church celebrates Mass daily at 10 am (except for Mondays) and normally stands open from 9 am to 11 am.

The pilgrimage tradition was revived in Dunfermline in the 20th century as a Catholic event. After some interruptions and changes of location, it resumed in 2015 and acquired an ecumenical dimension. This annual event takes place in June to celebrate the anniversary of Margaret's 1250 enshrinement.

St Andrews

The Way culminates at Scotland's foremost pilgrimage destination, St Andrews. How did the Fife settlement, known as Kilrymont until the late 11th century, come to be renamed after Andrew, the fisherman apostle? It is a complicated story, told fully in Bradley's excellent book: see page 70.

Andrew was martyred in AD 65 in Patras, Greece on the diagonal cross that later became the basis of the Saltire. Somehow St Andrew's relics (allegedly a tooth, arm-bone, kneecap and three fingers) were allegedly moved from Patras to Kilrymont. The story involves legend, Pictish public relations, church politics and nationalist feelings. Bradley concludes that the legends were probably invented in the 8th or 9th centuries after the cult of St Andrew reached eastern Scotland from Northumbria. He suggests that the Picts perhaps needed to trump the Gaelic cult of St Columba with an Apostolic saint.

Certainly St Andrews enjoyed 400 years of massive pilgrim popularity. In the 11th century, Queen Margaret was a frequent pilgrim and she donated a jewelled cross for the church altar. Along with Rome, Santiago and Canterbury, St Andrews became one of Europe's top four pilgrim destinations in terms of numbers. Its magnificent cathedral was among Europe's largest and grandest: see page 69. The town's layout, with two main streets converging on the cathedral, was designed to bring processions of pilgrims flocking to its cathedral. They were sometimes so densely thronged with pilgrims that a one-way system was needed.

Early map by John Geddy (c.1580)

Although the Reformation is normally blamed for ending the pilgrimage boom, Bradley demonstrates that the decline started early in the 16th century. This was partly because devotion to the Virgin Mary was supplanting the cult of the saint, and partly the rival demands of university students for accommodation were displacing those of pilgrims.

The arrival of Protestantism was, however, decisive. Scotland had been exposed to Lutheran influence since 1520. The preaching and martyrdom of Patrick Hamilton, slowly burned to death at the age of 24 turned many people away from Rome. He was the first of four men publicly burned for their Protestant beliefs between 1528 and 1558.

Statue of St Andrew

Another was George Wishart, who from 1543 was advocating justification by faith and Bible reading in the vernacular. He was betrayed to Cardinal David Beaton, Archbishop of St Andrews, arrested and imprisoned in the castle. After being condemned as a heretic, he was publicly hanged and burned at the stake in 1546. You can see the exact spot in the road just outside St Andrews Castle, marked with the initials GW.

In May 1546, 18 Protestant nobles and supporters of Wishart invaded the castle and stabbed Cardinal Beaton to death. They hung his body from the same window from which Beaton had so recently watched Wishart's death. They then occupied the castle for over a year, having consigned Beaton's corpse to the bottle dungeon, covered in salt to try to contain the stench.

Martyrs Monument

During the siege, they invited John Knox (1514-72) to come and tutor their children. The siege was half-hearted at first: Knox was allowed to come and go to Holy Trinity Church, where in 1547 he preached his first sermon, attacking the Catholic Church and the papacy. By July 1947 the siege had become warlike, with a bombardment from 21 French galleys. The occupants surrendered on condition that their lives were spared. However many (including Knox) were taken prisoner by the French and became galley slaves.

After 19 months of hardship and serious illness in the galley, Knox was eventually freed in 1549 and exiled abroad. After his return to Scotland in 1555, St Andrews emerged as the centre of Scottish Protestantism with Knox as its leader. He returned to preach in June 1559, again in Holy Trinity Church, fiercely condemning idolatry.

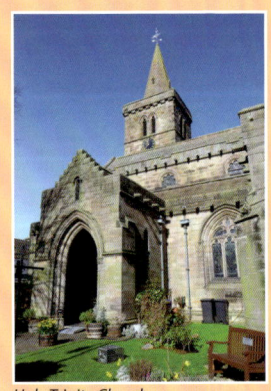
Holy Trinity Church

St Andrews Castle

The congregation carried out a brutal 'cleansing' of the church, and the town leaders then decided to remove idols and ornaments from other churches. Soon afterwards, the Parliament legally established Protestantism in Scotland.

The cathedral was seriously damaged by angry Protestants and had become disused by 1561. In the wake of the Reformation, St Andrews became a place of ruined churches, empty niches that had once housed statues and religious buildings that were defaced and decaying. Although there were many shocking individual cases, Scotland's Reformation was Europe's last, and relatively bloodless by comparison.

In modern times, a pilgrimage passes through the streets of St Andrews every Good Friday, an annual event that is supported by leaders of every local denomination. This peaceful and ecumenical tradition makes an inspiring contrast to the town's turbulent history.

East over the Cathedral ruins

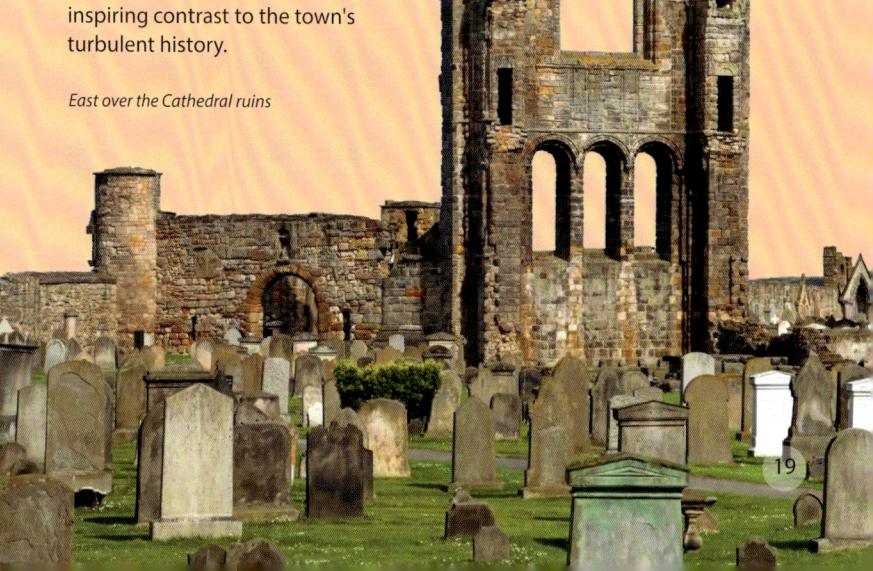

2·2 Miners and mining

Fife's coalfields have their orgins over 300 million years ago, at a time when the climate was hot and humid and the land covered by dense and luxuriant vegetation. Sea levels fluctuated and sedimentary materials were laid down, forming strata of calcium-rich limestone, sandstone and mudstone. Eventually the vegetation died and decomposed, forming thick beds of peat. Compressed by sedimentary layers, over a long period this turned into coal in seams up to 3 metres (10 feet) in thickness. Geological upheavals fractured and distorted the layers, often making the coal seams discontinuous and bringing some very close to the surface.

The foundations of the modern world were built on coal. It fuelled the Industrial Revolution from which later developments sprang. Fife was a leading producer within recent memory, with a range of pits – some opencast, some shallow and some deep. The legacy of the mining industry surrounds the route of the Way, especially in its western sections.

Coal was being mined in Fife at least 700 years ago. Small-scale opencast mining was widespread. A pit was operated by Cistercian monks for at least two centuries before the Reformation. In the 16th century it flooded and was closed. In the following century King James VI visited an early Fife mine and suspected treachery when he found himself emerging on to an artificial island in the Forth. In the 19th century, Sir Robert Preston created a more ambitious island as part of plan to exploit coal deposits near the water. Much later, ash from Longannet would be used to join it to the mainland.

Early coal mining was not confined to the south-west of the county. Between the 17th and 19th centuries, coal was extracted in the north-east with several mines situated around Ceres, which the Way passes through. This came at a high price in human hardship. In the early days, working conditions in the mines were among the worst in any sector in Britain. In some mines, the workers were effectively serfs – bound to the pit and sold as part of the business. This practice was finally abolished only in 1775.

However, conditions were little better in the early 19th century. Children as young as eight years old were sent to work underground. Women carried coal to the surface or dragged it upwards in carts, although hewing the coal was always seen as men's work. Reformers knew that Parliament was not ready to use the law to improve the working conditions of adult men, who were expected to look after themselves. However, they pressed for legislation to prevent the use of young children and to limit the hours worked by women. These changes had indirect benefits for male miners.

Mining was always a dangerous occupation. Collapses of the low tunnel ceilings were common in the early pits. Even after mine construction improved, other dangers persisted: collections of methane ('fire damp') created serious risks of explosion. The Valleyfield Pit was nicknamed 'gas tank' for its methane. At 4 am on 28 October 1939 a spark ignited gas and coal dust, causing the deaths of 35 miners and injuries to a further 26. It was one of Scotland's worst mining disasters. A statue depicting a mother and children waiting for news stands on a hill at High Valleyfield, and the Way passes a memorial obelisk near the B9037: see page 30.

Most of the early pits were small in scale and locally owned. In the later 19th century that began to change. The Fife Coal Company was formed in 1872 to develop mining around Kelty. Over time it acquired a number of pits in the surrounding area.

By the time of the World War 1, 20,000 miners were producing over 10 million tons from some 50 pits, mainly in the area between Dunfermline and Kirkcaldy. Fife had become the main centre of mining north of the Border, accounting for around 60% of Scotland's coal production.

Hopes for the future were high. In 1900 the Dunfermline Press estimated that the local coal reserves were sufficient to last for 600 years. A Royal Commission of 1905 went further: present output, it predicted, could be maintained for 930 years. In fact, the first half of the 20th century saw coal mining in Fife at its zenith. Despite the general recession after World War 1, which brought widespread unemployment to the mining villages, output later recovered. Some new pits opened, and World War 2 increased the demand for coal still further.

The newly-elected postwar Labour Government decided to place under public control the 'commanding heights of the economy'. Along with the gas, electricity and steel industries, the mines were to be nationalised.

Lindsay Pit, Kelty, early 20th century

Bronze statue outside New Kelty Library

Memorial to the Lindsay Colliery explosion (1957)

On 1 January 1947 the mines passed into the ownership of the National Coal Board. Naturally, the miners hoped for great improvements in their circumstances and, in part, their aspirations were met. A five-day week was introduced and pithead baths installed at those pits which did not have them.

Throughout the period, pits opened and closed as seams were exhausted or became uneconomic. By the 1950s, the industry was in general decline, although new pits were still opening. In Glenrothes, the new Rothes Colliery opened in 1957 with an intended lifespan of 100 years and an expectation that it would produce 5000 tons of coal per day. In fact, it had achieved only 1235 tons per day by 1960 and closed the following year – a result of geological problems and too much water. It was the greatest failure of the National Coal Board era in Scotland.

By the 1960s the decline was looking terminal, and by 1965 the last of the seven mines at Lochore closed. The deep mine at Longannet significantly outlasted all the other pits in Scotland. However, it too closed in 2002 following flooding. Although some minor opencast mining continued, traditional coal mining in Fife had ended. This resulted in very high unemployment in small towns and villages where there were few other sources of work.

Alongside unemployment, mining had brought widespread environmental degradation. Modern visitors to Lochore Meadows need real powers of imagination to visualise how it must have appeared when the mines closed. The loch itself had been drained in 1792. Over time, lagoons of sludge replaced its waters. Spoil heaps (bings) dominated the skyline. An ambitious programme of improvement started almost immediately. Today the landscape of the whole coalfield has been restored, leaving few clues as to how it looked during the years of the first Industrial Age.

Fife was a place of relatively small mining communities – close-knit and distinctive. Many had a Miners' Institute, as walkers will see on the Way at Kinglassie and Lochore. These offered a range of social, recreational and educational opportunities. An American journalist visiting at the beginning of the 20th century commented on the impressive library at Kelty.

Heavy drinking, especially of beer, was a feature of some mining areas. The Temperance movement made strong efforts to limit the impact of drunkenness. An interesting approach was the Gothenburg movement, which set up public houses on a Swedish model. These served unadulterated drink and devoted their profits to the public good in the form of street lighting, recreation grounds and similar facilities. Three 'Goth' pubs can be seen along the Way; the Goth Tavern in Newmills, the No 1 Goth in Kelty and the Red Goth in Lochore.

The mining communities also supported radical action, and strikes were common in the 19th century. The General Strike paralysed Britain for nine days in May 1926. It had arisen from the miners' strike that protested against the coal owners trying to reduce wages and increase hours. In the event neither strike achieved its objectives.

A later miners' strike in 1974 was credited with bringing about the downfall of Edward Heath's Conservative Government. The most famous miners' strike of the relatively recent past was that of 1984/85. Although little remained of the industry in Fife, it was strongly supported in its mining communities. However, it eventually collapsed, leading to the closure of almost all remaining mines in the UK.

Support for militant industrial action went in parallel with support for radical politics. Britain's first Communist MP, Willie Gallacher, was elected for the West Fife constituency in 1935 and managed to retain his seat until 1950. The Communists also enjoyed some success in elections to Fife Council. When Willie Clarke resigned his seat in 2016, he was the last Communist councillor in the UK. The Way passes the Visitor Centre at Lochore Meadows that was named after him.

Labour politicians have also been strong influencers over the years in west Fife. Jenny Lee, a leading Labour figure of the 1960s, came from Lochgelly. Gordon Brown was brought up in Kirkcaldy, the birthplace of Adam Smith (*Wealth of Nations*). He represented the area as its Labour Member of Parliament for 32 years from 1983 to 2015. In 1997, jointly with Mick McGahey of the National Union of Mineworkers, he unveiled the David Annand memorial sculpture that stands outside Kelty's Community Centre. He was also famously the longest-serving Chancellor of the Exchequer (1997-2007) in modern times, and Prime Minister from 2007 to 2010.

West Fife no longer looks like a mining landscape, but along the Way, you'll see statues, memorials, and plaques. St Ninians displays an avenue of heavy machinery: see page 45. The huge former opencast mine at Westfield, once one of Europe's largest, is now a 1000-acre site set to develop energy from waste.

At Lochore Meadows, even the children's playpark celebrates the mining heritage and the winding gear of the former Mary Pit stands nearby.

Winding gear from the Mary Pit, Lochore Meadows

2·3 Habitats and wildlife

If you are keen to spot wildlife, it's worth carrying binoculars – not only for birds, but also to see larger animals from a distance without disturbing them. Try to move quietly and be aware that many animals are more active around dawn and dusk.

Common blues, male

The Way starts beside the shores of the Forth, then moves into rural sections passing mainly through farmland and golf courses, with riverine interludes and visits to lochs and reservoirs. Aside from a few small patches of woodland, the three main habitats are:

- coastal
- farmland and hedgerow
- inland water

Coastal

Wherever you start from, the first part of the Way runs along the shore of the Firth of Forth. In spring and summer, this estuary is rich in wildflowers, with deep yellow cowslips contrasting with magenta flowers of bloody cranesbill, especially around Carlingnose nature reserve (near North Queensferry). The abandoned jetty, a relic from wartime, has become a great nesting site for terns. These elegant silvery-grey and white birds are graceful in flight and often hover over the water before diving for fish: see the photo on page 25.

The white flowers of common scurvygrass may be less colourful, but the plant tells an interesting story. Its dark green succulent leaves are rich in vitamin C, which is vital to human health but which we can't create for ourselves. Before the importance of fresh food was understood, up to 50% of sailors on long voyages used to become seriously ill or die of scurvy – a disease easily treated with any source of vitamin C. By the late 18th century, British sailors were given daily rations of lemon juice or dried scurvygrass.

Bloody cranesbill

Common tern

Gannet

Sea buckthorn

Another great source of vitamin C is sea buckthorn with its rich orange berries, sharp spines and useful ability to tolerate salt spray. It's a feature of the Valleyfield lagoons that you may walk through just after Culross.

The lagoons were created from ash, a byproduct of Longannet power station, and the reclaimed land has become a haven for wildlife. Near the shore you will see waders such as oystercatchers, redshanks, curlews, and many seabirds. In summer, look out for the common blue butterfly.

Eider duck

Out on the Firth, look for eider ducks, fulmars – a small cousin of the albatross – and gannets. Eider ducks often float in large rafts, feeding on shellfish and making their distinctive cooing calls. Gannets are the elite athletes among seabirds: they climb to heights of 30 m (100 ft), fold their wings and dive-bomb their prey at speeds of over 50 mph (80 kph).

Oystercatcher

Brown hare

Field vole

Farmland and hedgerow

Much of the Way runs through farmland which is rich in small mammals such as field mice, voles and shrews, with chances to see the birds that prey on them, such as kestrels, sparrowhawks and buzzards. Farmland is also home to larger mammals, including the brown hare and the occasional roe deer. Above the fields, look out (and listen) for skylarks – resident year-round, but almost unseen and unheard in winter. Spring and summer are when the males soar to amazing heights and fill the air with their thrilling, melodious song. Often the bird flies so high as to be invisible against the sky, but its song is unmistakable.

Skylark

Ravens are the largest member of the corvid (crow) family, with large black bodies and heavy bills. They form monogamous pairs that adopt a territory and defend it from intruders. They are omnivorous, eating twice their body weight daily, and their intelligence makes them good collaborators. Only if food is scarce will they gather with other ravens in a group called a conspiracy. Once you've heard their distinctive call, you will find them easy to identify: it sounds like a raucous croak: *cruk-cruk*. They often soar above crags and cliffs and are common around Drumcarrow Craig: see page 64.

Hedgerows are easily overlooked, but they provide vital shelter, as well as food sources, for small mammals and birds. Early summer brings hawthorn with its fragrant white flowers and pink dogrose whose flowers later ripen to rose hips. Gorse is very common and its yellow flowers appear in almost any month, smelling of almond or coconut – opinions differ.

Wren *Yellowhammer*

The bird life in hedgerows is mainly small, with sizes ranging from the tiny wren upwards. Recognise the wren by its rapid, darting flight and cocked tail, and by its loud alarm call if you disturb it. Warblers including blackcaps dive in and out of dense vegetation, where they may nest, and rarer beauties include the yellowhammer and goldfinch.

Inland water

The Way visits a number of bodies of fresh water: it crosses Loch Fitty and passes the eastern end of Clatto Reservoir (built in 1874 to supply water to Dundee), where there's a hide overlooking the water. It goes around the northern shore of Loch Ore for a mile, where you will see larger birds, including mallards and tufted ducks, cormorants and mute swans. The nature reserve is centred on two sheltered ponds at its western end, well worth a visit: you may spot coots, moorhens and grebes, and, if you're lucky, a kingfisher.

Rivers and streams attract bird life and in fast-moving rivers and near rapids you may see dippers – a dark brown bird with a smart white breast and aquatic tendencies. It plunges in fearlessly to feed on tiny fish, molluscs and tadpoles. Look out also for the bobbing of wagtails, both pied (black-and-white) and grey (with yellow underparts).

Kingfisher

3 Culross

The Culross of today is a tribute to a century of conservation efforts by the National Trust for Scotland. Its famous buildings include the 1597 Palace with its authentic mustard-yellow render and wooden shutters (open daily from March to October). Its interior features painted ceilings, tiny rooms and narrow passageways. The walled garden is open year-round and its raised beds illustrate historic gardening techniques. They are in active use and their organic produce sells well locally.

Typical houses in Culross

The A-listed Town House was built in 1626 to replace an earlier tolbooth on the same site, and is strikingly Scottish medieval in style. Its symmetry is extended even to the twin access staircases with a clock tower centred over them. The Abbey and monastery ruins stand on the hillside above the village: read more on page 15. The Way visits them en route out of the village.

Culross is noted for its tranquil 16-17th century ambience, with unspoiled cobbled streets and narrow wynds. It was featured often in the TV series Outlander. Take time to wander around its centre and soak up the historic atmosphere. Afterwards, for more tangible refreshment visit the Biscuit Café, up an alley beside the Town House or Bessie's Café at the Palace. For visitor information on Culross, visit *bit.ly/RR-culross*.

Culross Palace

3·1a Culross to Dunfermline

Distance 8·7 miles 14·0 km
Terrain over half on pavement or roads, with the rest on well-marked footpaths
Grade gentle gradients with a mild overall gain in altitude; two short climbs
Food and drink Culross (cafés), Cairneyhill (shops), Dunfermline (wide range)
Summary undemanding walk from the historic conservation village of Culross, with pleasant views and some further points of interest along the way

Culross	2·8		2·4		3·5	Dunfermline
0	4·5	Torry tunnel	3·9	Cairneyhill Church	5·6	8·7

- At the Culross West car park, ignore the Fife Coastal Path noticeboard and look instead for the the Fife Pilgrim Way noticeboard near the children's play park. With your back to the Firth of Forth, go north across Culross's main street and up the road to Culross Palace: for visit information, see **bit.ly/RR-palace**.

- About 75 m after the palace entrance, turn left on the cobbled street (Back Causeway) which heads uphill to Culross Abbey, becoming first Tanhouse Brae, then Kirk Street.

- After 350 m of this road, a FPW waymarker points you to turn right on Newgate, just before the abbey ruins. First keep ahead for a look at Abbey Church which is well worth a visit: see **bit.ly/RR-culr**.

Tanhouse Brae

Signboard at the Culross start

- Afterwards, return to the waymarker and go down Newgate that bends downhill between stone walls until within 300 m you reach the main road.
- Turn left to follow the pavement for 450 m, passing the ruins of a chapel dedicated to St Mungo, where the altar is still visible.
- About 100 m after the chapel, between the two bus stops look for the waymarked path between two houses and cross the road to take it (mile 0·9). Stop, look and listen at the unmanned crossing and when it's safe, cross over the railway line.
- Turn left onto the well-marked footpath which is shared with the Fife Coastal Path (FCP) for the next couple of miles. The tarmac path runs between the Valleyfield lagoons on your right and the railway on your left.
- After 0·9 mile (1·4 km) bear right up a ramp to re-cross the railway by a high tubular footbridge. On the far side, descend the ramp and turn right (unsigned) down the steps to rejoin the path on your right, now heading east again.
- At mile 2, the footpath reaches the road and the FPW turns right along it, joining the B9037 within 200 m, soon after the memorial to Valleyfield Colliery (1908-1978).

Unmanned railway crossing

Valleyfield Colliery memorial

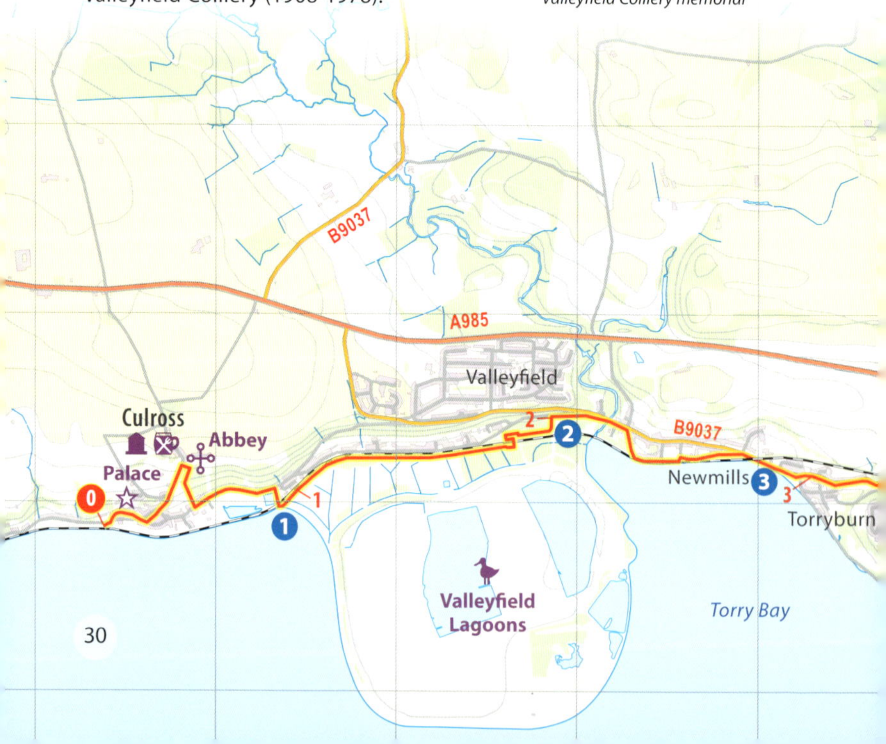

- Cross the Bluther Burn and 100 m afterwards turn right onto a footpath towards the Firth. After 400 m it joins a lane that meanders past houses before bringing you back to the B9037 through Newmills.
- Go through the pedestrian Torry Tunnel towards Torryburn, and at its far end cross the B9037 to see the small plaque set into the ground to commemorate Lilias Adie (1640-1704), who was killed for witchcraft.
- At mile 2·9 the FCP bears off right along the shore, but the FPW keeps to the main road through Torryburn. It climbs gently among the trees, with the Torry Burn below to your right for half a mile.
- At the top of the ascent (mile 3·9) bear right on the path through a metal gate at which cyclists dismount.
- After 600 m the path emerges at the main road (A985). Cross the road with care and take the path directly opposite (Muirside Lane).
- After 150 m bear left along the path, which after a further 250 m crosses the railway line and continues to the main road (A994).
- Turn right to follow the pavement through Cairneyhill for 800 m to mile 5·2. Opposite Carneyhill Parish Church turn left up the track to your left (Hilton Road) past a few houses.
- The track soon narrows to a path that bends right around the edge of the woods, then detours around a garden (Hilton) before becoming a well-defined track.
- Follow this track gently downhill passing farm buildings before reaching Crossford at mile 6·3.
- Where the track meets Lundin Road cross straight over and follow Kirkwood Crescent among the houses. After 270 m turn left up the road to Knockhouse Farm.

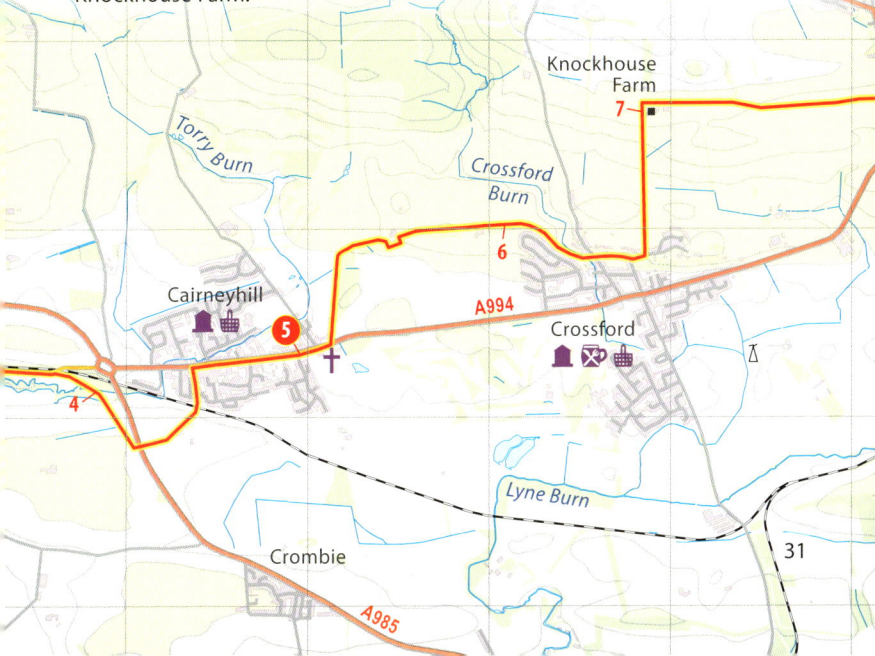

- Climb the hill to Knockhouse Farm (mile 7). Where various paths cross the Way, turn right and pass through the farmyard: be aware of livestock.
- Follow this path east for 0·9 miles (1·5 km) until you meet the A907 road. Cross straight over it and continue into Cameron Street. At its end (mile 8·1), turn right into Maitland Street.
- After 200 m reach the A994 and cross over into Pittencrief Park. ❶ Walk down the main path, with playpark on the right and a possible detour left and uphill to a statue of Andrew Carnegie who donated the park.
- After 270 m reach the Glen Pavilion with Peacock Rooms. Unless visiting its café, turn left at a green fingerpost and pass public toilets on the broad path that goes under an arch. Pass a path to a Japanese garden and cross the valley by a bridge. The sign on the right is for a detour down to Wallace's Well where William Wallace is thought to have taken refuge in 1303.

Left turn at the fingerpost

- However there is a fine viewpoint on a much shorter detour if instead you visit Malcolm Canmore's Tower by going up the unsigned rocky steps to the left. The tower was first mentioned about AD 1070 when the widowed King Malcolm III married Margaret: see page 15. It features in the coat of arms and Latin motto of Dunfermline. From the remains of its base there are excellent views including east to Dunfermline Abbey. See page 41 for a town plan.
- Afterwards continue in the same direction on the descent path which has more information at its foot, and an artist's impression of its impregnable location. From here it's only about 100 m to exit the park and the climb to the abbey.

Dunfermline Abbey

- The FPW signboard is just to the right of the steps leading up to the abbey. At this point the FPW from North Queensferry joins your route from the right. Depending on your plans and time of day, this may be the moment to visit the abbey: see *bit.ly/RR-dunf*. Otherwise head east to reach the town centre with accommodation, eateries and public transport.

Dunfermline bus station is a hub for Stagecoach bus routes including the X55 to Edinburgh, the X24 to Glenrothes, and the X24 to Cupar and St Andrews. The 8A connects Dunfermline with Culross. Dunfermline City railway station is on the Fife Circle and there's a further station (Dunfermline Queen Margaret) near mile 10·4. To continue the Way, see the town plan on page 41 and directions on page 42.

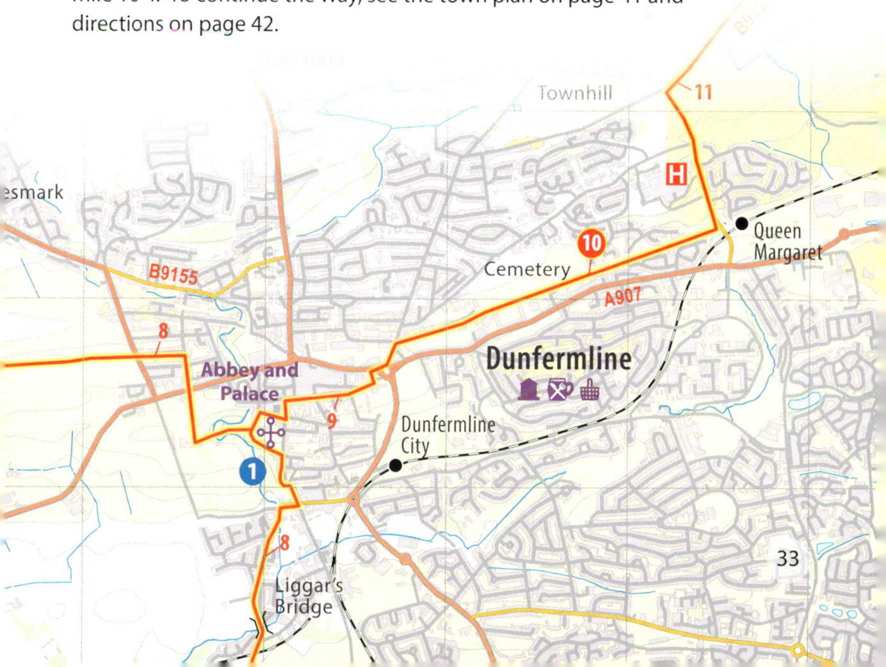

3.1b North Queensferry to Dunfermline

Distance	8·7 miles 14·0 km
Terrain	over half on pavement or roads, with the rest on well-marked footpaths
Grade	mostly gentle gradients with short climbs near the beginning; a mild overall gain in altitude
Food and drink	Inverkeithing (shops, cafés and civic centre) and Dunfermline (wide range)
Summary	undemanding walk with some fine views of Inverkeithing Bay and over the Firth of Forth, especially after Inverkeithing

North Queensferry 0 — 2·6 — 4·2 Inverkeithing Centre — 3·4 — 5·5 — 2·7 — Douglas Bank 4·3 — **Dunfermline** 8·7

Queensferry takes its name from Queen Margaret, the wife of King Malcolm III of Scotland. She established the village to ensure regular ferry crossings across the Firth of Forth for the benefit of pilgrims travelling to St Andrews. Margaret is thought to have arrived here in 1068, and to have regularly used the ferry crossing when travelling between the then capital Dunfermline, and Edinburgh Castle. From about this time, the crossing became known as the Queen's Ferry. Margaret died in 1093 and made her final journey by ferry to Dunfermline Abbey. The ferry continued to ply until 1964 when it was superseded by the opening of the first road bridge.

- If you arrived by train, follow the brown fingerpost signs from North Queensferry station, go steeply down Ferryhill Road and across Old Kirk Road, towards the former Albert Hotel.
- Start at the FPW signboard on Battery Road, near the Forth Bridge. There are information boards about the Way and the ancient history of this landing point for pilgrims including Queen Margaret: see page 16. Enjoy great views of the three bridges as they diverge from here across the Forth, and perhaps walk down to the water's edge to consider the pilgrims who landed here by ferry.

Signboard at the North Quensferry start

- With your back to the Forth, turn left up Battery Road and follow the road around to the right, heading north uphill past Post Office Lane. Just 40 m later cross Old Kirk Road, and on its far side follow the fingerpost along a cobbled path marked by a circular plaque set into the ground
- The path is shared with the Fife Coastal Path so expect to follow signage for FPW and/or FCP. It soon takes you underneath the splendid Forth Bridge, carrying the railway high above, with clear views of its immense stone pillars and fine Victorian engineering.
- Follow this path as it climbs gently with several changes of surface and enters Carlingnose Point Nature Reserve (Scottish Wildlife Trust). Info boards explain various distinctive forms of wildlife, including the repurposing of the disused World War 1 jetty as a nesting site for terns.
- Continue through the nature reserve down to the bay and beach. Near the start of the beach, at the end of a stone wall with balcony there's a square plate on your left. It's a memorial to a 21 year old army officer killed while protecting his men from a grenade during training for World War 1.
- Continue past the beach and at mile 1 reach Ardalanish where there's a bench and viewpoint over the Forth and its islands, with the distinctive elephant-back of Arthur's Seat, Edinburgh distant to the south-east. After you round the headland, you hug the coast of Inner Bay with Inverkeithing visible on its far side.

South over the Forth, with 1964 road bridge at right

- Near the end of the path, cross over a zigzag metal ramp, soon seeing and hearing the machinery of Robertson Metals Recycling.
- At mile 1·6 emerge onto Cruickness Road, passing two gateways into the recycling plant, with possible large vehicle traffic. Where the road ends, turn right for 90 m and turn right along Hope Street (B981).

- After 300 m the road goes under a railway bridge, and you continue uphill for a further 500 m into Inverkeithing. You reach shops and the Inverkeithing Civic Centre, set back on your right. To its left is the Grey Friars Hospitium, a medieval building used as a pilgrimage hostelry.
- Returning to Hope Street, just after the Millbarista Café reach a mini-roundabout where you turn left up Hill Street. It climbs steeply out of Inverkeithing for about 500 m, levels out and crosses Manse Road, then descends to cross a bridge over the M90 motorway.
- Immediately turn right at the T-junction and then after 40 m turn left into Lothians View to walk uphill again, with no pavement at first. After 400 m you pass some houses and a comms mast, enjoying good views over the Forth and its bridges to the left. There's a World War 2 concrete pillbox in the field on your right.

Mercat Cross, Inverkeithing

West over Rosyth on the descent from Castlandhill

- After the Castlandhill houses, the road becomes grassy and runs down beside a field edge, with Rosyth's giant blue crane soon visible ahead. About halfway down the descent, follow a signed left-right dogleg.

- Near the foot of the hill, make a right-left dogleg to descend the final grassy slope to Ferrytoll Road. Turn right and follow its pavement for 500 m to reach a large roundabout near the entrance to Rosyth Dockyard.

- Leaving the roundabout to your left, take the second exit into Hilton Rd. Follow it for 350 m, then turn right into Wilson Way, signed 'Rosyth FC'. After 150 m turn left to continue past the Football Club.

- Walk past the pitches on your left slightly uphill. After nearly 400 m turn left on a public footpath that within 200 m turns right to reach the busy A985.

> **Rosyth Dockyard**
> Rosyth dockyard has been an important maritime resource since it was established in 1909. It was one of the Royal Navy's largest dockyards, with a capacity for both shipbuilding and repair. Its northerly location helped it to serve the naval fleet which was based in Orkney in both World Wars. The dockyard could meet the needs of large battleships, smaller boats and submarines.
>
> The Navy largely moved out in 1996, but still maintains a small presence as HMS Caledonia. The dockyard now belongs to Babcock International, and its focus is on maintaining and modernising vessels, while serving as a dock for visiting cruise ships.

- Turn left and follow the pavement (on the left) beside the busy A985. This is the least pleasant section of the walk, and it's a pleasure to leave the traffic noise after 0·7 mile/1·2 km. For safety, stay on the pavement until after you've crossed the Hilton Road junction and you are opposite the turning at mile 5·7.

- Cross the A985 with care and turn right up the road signed for Douglasbank Cemetery. After 270 m pass the Douglas Bank Lodge at the cemetery entrance. To visit its Commonwealth War Graves, enter the cemetery and go up to the left.

- From the cemetery entrance turn left on the path with a green sign for Leckerstone and Grange Road. It climbs beside the cemetery boundary, with some good views over the beech hedge. Soon the path reaches more open ground and within 700 m of the cemetery, reach a small metal gate ahead.

- Here you leave the path (which turns right to pass around the wood) and go through the gate into deciduous woodland. Follow the path for 150 m through the wood and exit on an avenue lined with hedgerow. This bears left to another small wood on your left, and you soon emerge at a T-junction with a potholed farm road.

- Turn right along the road for 450 m to reach Wester Gellet Farm. Turn left on another farm road which undulates; from its upper part there are views to your right of the Forth bridges with Arthur's Seat more distant to the left.
- About 550 m after the farm, reach the B9156 which you will follow for one mile (1·6 km) all the way into Dunfermline. Enjoy your first glimpse of Dunfermline Abbey ahead.
- At first there is a narrow path on the right side of the road only, but after 900 m you approach Liggar's Bridge over a stream, and must cross to the left for pavement.
- Continue into Dunfermline, past Dunfermline Rugby Club on your left, the B9156 bends sharply to the right. Follow it around the bend and within 90 m reach a crossroads with traffic lights.
- Turn left to walk up Moodie Street, and after 100 m bear left on a footpath which passes through the car park of the Andrew Carnegie Birthplace Museum, a building gifted to Dunfermline by Andrew's wife, Louise Whitfield Carnegie. For information about the museum including visiting hours, see the panel.

Andrew Carnegie

Andrew Carnegie (1835-1919) is Dunfermline's most famous son. Born in a weaver's cottage, he and his family emigrated to America in 1848. There he worked hard and showed great entrepreneurial skill. Investing mainly in the steel industry, he became the richest man in the world. In 1901 he embarked on philanthropy on an enormous scale, setting up over 2500 public libraries, places of higher education and concert halls. By the time he died, he had given away $350 million – equivalent to $6.5 billion today. Carnegie repeatedly returned to Dunfermline and donated large amounts to improve the town and its environs. The Way passes Dunfermline's Carnegie Library and, later, its Carnegie Hall. Visit his birthplace, now a museum: entry is free, details at www.carnegiebirthplace.com.

- Just beyond the museum, join St Margaret Street and after 70 m turn left into Monastery Street. Follow the broad path straight ahead which goes up beside the ruins of the monastery and palace to reach the Abbey within 200 m. The impressive two-storey stonework to your right is the surviving south range walls of the refectory hall.
- On the left, notice the blue circular plaque explaining the role of the palace as birthplace of many royals including Charles 1 in 1600. Go under the arch in the monastery gateway and veer right to reach the FPW signboard just in front of the steps up to the Abbey.
- At this point the FPW from Culross joins your route from the left. Depending on your plans and the time of day, this may be the moment to visit the abbey nave. (As of 2024 the palace and refectory had been closed by Historic Environment Scotland.)
- Otherwise head east to reach the town centre with accommodation, eateries and railway and bus stations. For transport connections from Dunfermline, see page 33. To continue the Way, see the town plan on page 41 and directions on page 42.

East over Pittencrieff Park

South range of the refectory, Abbey at right

Dunfermline

Dunfermline has a population of about 58,000 and became Scotland's eighth city in 2022. It is steeped in history and served as Scotland's capital for much of the Middle Ages. In about 1072 Queen (Saint) Margaret, wife of Malcolm III, invited the Benedictines to set up a new community in the town, thus helping to tilt Scottish Christianity towards Rome.

A new abbey church was inaugurated in 1128. Its Impressive Norman nave, similar in style to Durham Cathedral, is still in use. The original choir was replaced by a new gothic revival building in 1821. It serves as Dunfermline's parish church.

City Chambers roofline

The Abbey was the Scottish royal mausoleum between 1093 and 1420. Robert the Bruce (reigned 1306-29) was the last of seven Scottish kings to be buried here. His remains lie beneath the pulpit of the abbey church, and his name appears on the tower of the new church.

The foundations of Queen Margaret's original church are buried under the present church's nave but the refectory can still be seen along with the ruins of later abbey buildings and the gatehouse of the palace. As a large abbey, Dunfermline had a guest house which was probably built in the 13th century. It was later taken over by Scottish kings as a palace and was rebuilt at various times, most recently by James IV and James VI.

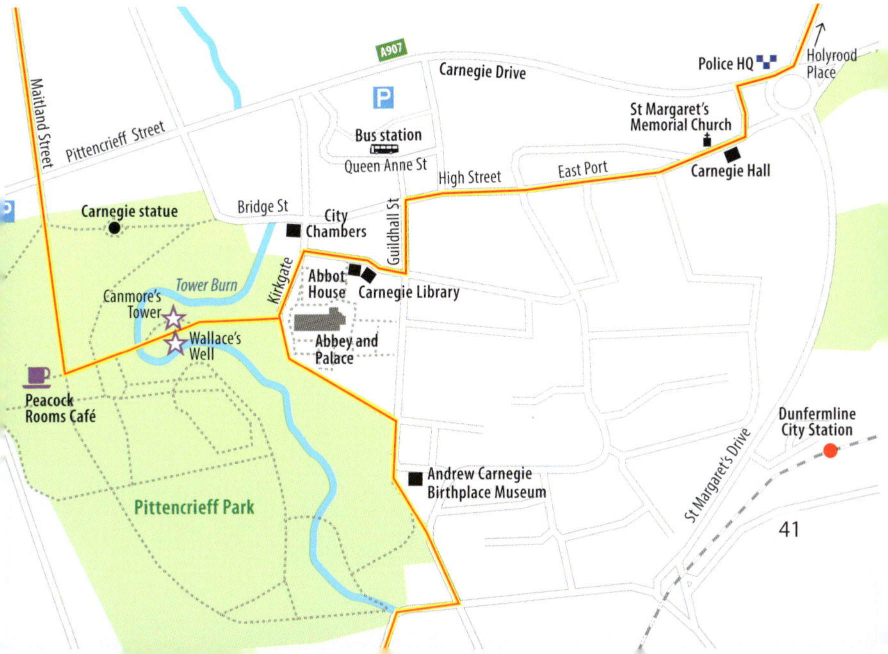

3·2 Dunfermline to Crosshill

		43	47

Distance 11·1 miles 17·9 km
Terrain about 30% on pavement or roads, with the rest on well-marked footpaths
Grade mostly fairly flat after a short climb out of Dunfermline up to Kingseat, then a longer one (to 210 m) from Loch Fitty; gentle descent to Crosshill
Food and drink Dunfermline (wide range), Lochore Centre (café)
Summary walk through the heart of Fife's mining areas, the legacy of collieries and their machinery still visible; near the end, the Way passes Loch Ore and its Country Park Centre

Dunfermline	3·3		4·1		3·7	Crosshill
8·7	5·3	Kingseat	6·6	M90	6·0	19·8

- To resume the Way, return to the FPW signboard at the abbey, this time turning north up St Catherine's Wynd.
- After 100 m, the Way turns right into Maygate but you may first want a closer look at the landmark Scots baronial City Chambers ahead on the left: see the photo on page 41.
- Afterwards, continue on Maygate, within 70 m reaching the Abbot House: see the panel opposite.
- Soon after Abbot House pass Dunfermline Carnegie Library (with café), and then turn left uphill into Guildhall Street, a pedestrianised area. After 100 m it meets the High Street at a junction marked by the Mercat Cross ahead.
- The Way turns right along the High Street, but to reach the bus station go ahead uphill past the Mercat Cross and turn left into Queen Anne Street.
- After the High Street and pedestrian area ends, keep ahead on East Port for a further 400 m. You pass Viewfield Baptist and Holy Trinity Episcopal Churches on the right.
- After the road bends left, pass (or visit) St Margaret's Memorial Church on the left and Dunfermline's very own Carnegie Hall up to the right.
- Before a double roundabout, turn left towards the busy Carnegie Drive dual carriageway, and use its pedestrian crossing. On its far side, walk past the police HQ and bear left into Holyrood Place at mile 9·3.
- After 120 m reach a mini-roundabout, where you bear right into Leys Park Road. Follow its pavement to the end of the free public car park, then bear right on a cycleway. It follows a former railway trackbed, soon passing between a cemetery and a football stadium.

Abbot House entrance

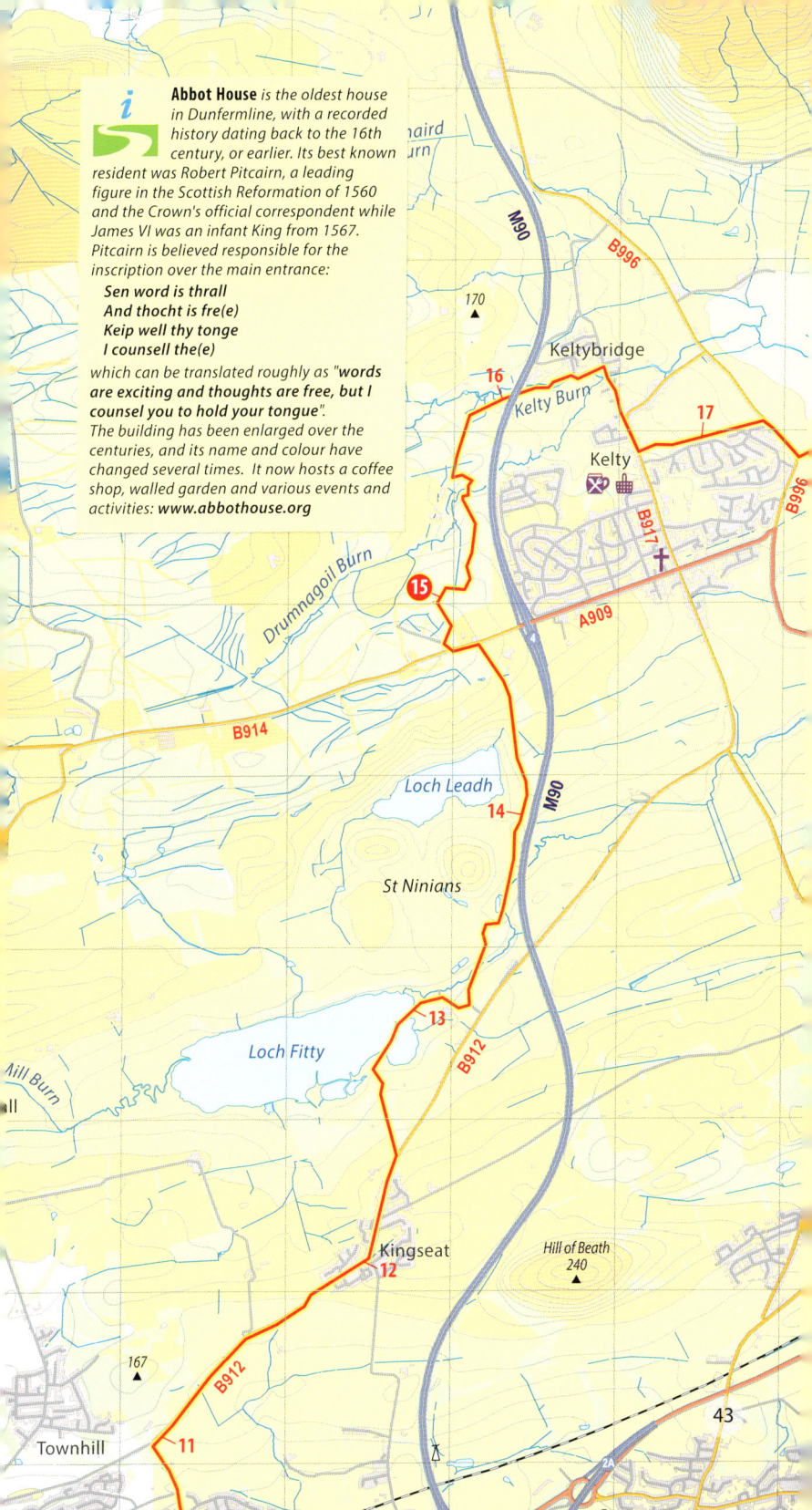

Abbot House is the oldest house in Dunfermline, with a recorded history dating back to the 16th century, or earlier. Its best known resident was Robert Pitcairn, a leading figure in the Scottish Reformation of 1560 and the Crown's official correspondent while James VI was an infant King from 1567. Pitcairn is believed responsible for the inscription over the main entrance:

Sen word is thrall
And thocht is fre(e)
Keip well thy tonge
I counsell the(e)

which can be translated roughly as "*words are exciting and thoughts are free, but I counsel you to hold your tongue*". The building has been enlarged over the centuries, and its name and colour have changed several times. It now hosts a coffee shop, walled garden and various events and activities: www.abbothouse.org

- After nearly a mile (1·4 km) the path ends at a T-junction with a signpost at the B912 road. Turn left and walk uphill on its left pavement, passing the Queen Margaret Hospital and going over a mini-roundabout.
- After half a mile (800 m) uphill, the B912 turns right (for Kingseat and Kelty) at an apparent T-junction with a minor road. Just before the road junction, turn right onto the signed tarmac cycleway and follow it for over a mile into Kingseat, gently uphill.

Cemetery at mile 9·5

- The hill ahead to the right is Hill of Beath (240 m/790 ft), which lies beyond the M90. As you approach Kingseat look also behind you (south) for views of the Forth and its three bridges: see page 35.
- Just before Kingseat the cycleway joins the pavement and a panel explains the role of Colin Smith (1952-2013) in creating the walkway/cycleway, and shows where the local collieries were.
- Go through the village, which has panels about its mining heritage and another map showing local pits.
- Soon after the village ends, turn left off the road on a gated track at mile 12·4. Descend to and through a gate and walk about 700 m down to Loch Fitty.
- At the shore, turn right to follow the path across the end of the loch on a narrow causeway which gives great views over the loch, but is quite exposed in high winds.

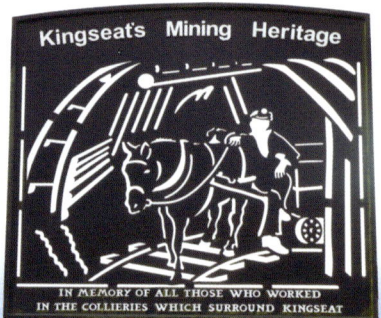
Causeway across Loch Fitty, frozen in winter

Avenue of heavy machinery

- Afterwards the track reaches a T-junction where you turn right past the stables. Within 200 m reach a junction where you turn left to the gated entrance to St Ninians. This is a huge area formerly devoted to opencast mining, reinventing itself as a health and wellness destination: see www.stninianswellness.com.
- Go through the gate and follow the road, on tarmac at first, later on a loose-surfaced track. Over the next 1·4 miles (2·2 km) it descends before climbing steadily past the artifical hill of St Ninians East: see the panel for a possible detour. You pass an enormous empty tarmac area, sometimes used as a venue for entertainment events.
- The Way runs very close to the M90 in this section, and its traffic noise will be all too obvious, but is short-lived. Keep ahead (north) past the end of Loch Leadh to reach the B914 road at mile 14·7.
- Turn left along the B914 pavement for 180 m to reach Blairadam Forestry car park with its monument to all who worked in the Kelty collieries. Turn right down the side of the car park and onto a woodland path that descends gently.
- After 600 m reach a crossroads: ignore the sign to Kelty via M90 and keep straight on. Follow the path downhill, soon crossing a wooden bridge over Drumnagoil Burn. The path soon comes to a T-junction at mile 15·6.
- Turn right and after 130 m look for the brick wall on your left with a plaque depicting the Beast of Blairadam, a mythical huge cat-like beast that was said to roam the forest: see page 46. After a further 200 m at a crossroads turn right as signed (or cut the corner).
- Within 300 m cross the M90 motorway by its underpass. Carry on along the path which becomes a track as it descends gently into Keltybridge, with the Kelty Burn on your right and some views of the hills to the left.

> **St Ninians East**
> The three artificial hills to your left rise to 177, 170 and 181 m (from west to east) and were part of an ambitious project designed by landscape architect Charles Jencks that was abandoned in 2013. St Ninians East (181 m) is also known as the 'walnut whip' because of the spiral paths from north and south that intertwine as they ascend. At the top there are art forms and an avenue of mining machinery. The spiral paths make for easy walking but you could climb the steep grassy slope instead.

Brick wall inscribed with the Beast of Blairadam

- About 550 m after the M90, reach a junction with the Main Street: turn right, and descend to cross the Kelty Burn by its road bridge.

- Stay on the pavement, crossing a road junction and still climbing. Opposite the convenience store with ATM, turn left to walk down Whitegates Terrace. The sign is not obvious, so look out for this turning just 500 m after you join Main Street.

- Whitegates Terrace soon ends but the Way continues ahead on a channel-fenced path which descends to the Great North Road (B996) after 600 m. Note the large pole depicting a miner and symbols on your left at the end of the path.

- Turn right to walk beside the B996 and leave it after 300 m at the large blue sign for Lochore Meadows. Turn left down the access road into the country park.

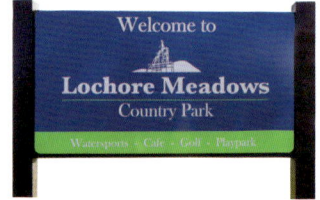

- Follow the path through the car park and after 500 m reach a junction where you bear left.

- After a further 300 m, turn left to cross the River Ore by a metal footbridge. About 450 m beyond the footbridge, at a T-junction turn right along a broad track (Benarty Road).

- After 350 m reach Benarty Bay car park. Go through the gate and after 90 m, bear right down the path to your right.

- This runs around the shore of the loch for about a mile until you come to the Willie Clarke Visitor Centre at mile 19·4. The centre displays local information (look up to see the time line running from 300 million years ago to the present day) in its café. This car park may make a good rendez-vous for a lift.

- Alternatively, continue to Crosshill by keeping ahead along the path at the side of the road. After 60 m it divides: ignore the path to the right that goes down to the shore, instead forking left along the side of the road.

East over Lochore Meadows Country Park

- Walk past the ruins of Lochore Castle and emerge to meet the main road (B920) at a small roundabout. Turn left for Crosshill's shops and bus stops (for either Glenrothes or Dunfermline) or turn right (south) for Lochgelly's station just over a mile away (1·8 km).
- From Crosshill, Stagecoach bus number 31 will take you south-west back to Dunfermline, or north-east onward to Glenrothes.

Ruins of Lochore Castle

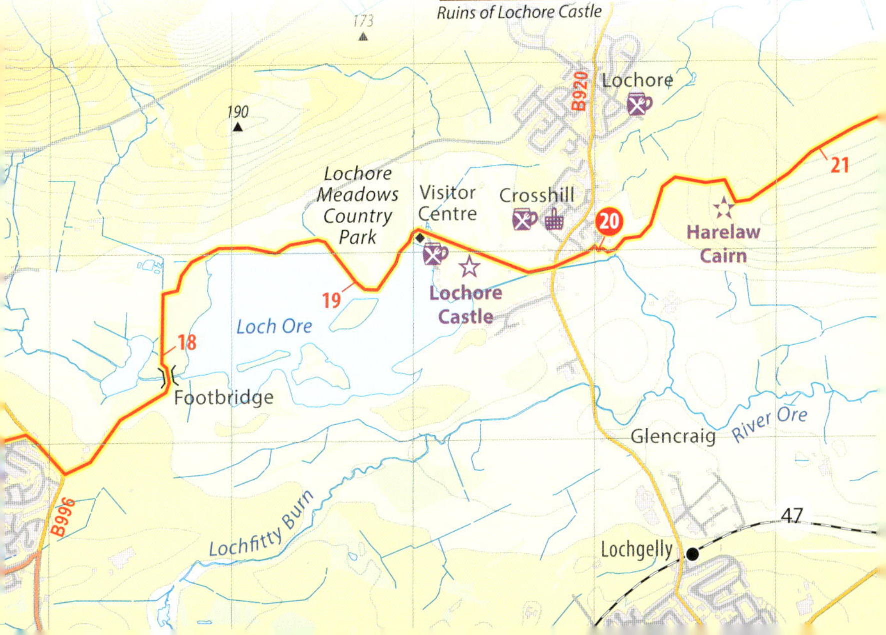

3·3 Crosshill to Leslie

Distance 8·0 miles 12·9 km
Terrain about 30% on pavement or roads, with the rest on well-marked footpaths
Grade mostly gentle gradients with one short steep climb out of Kinglassie
Food and drink Lochore Centre (café), Crosshill (shops), Kinglassie (café and shops), Leslie (cafés and shops)
Summary a pleasant and undemanding walk with a two-mile stretch on the B921 pavement; some unexpected vistas, especially after the climb out of Kinglassie

Crosshill	2·6		2·1		3·3	Leslie
19·8	4·2	B921	3·4	Kinglassie	5·3	27·

- From Crosshill's roundabout, make a left-right dogleg into Park St and follow it for 220 m to where the houses end. Look up to the right for a small grassy mound which you climb to a brown heritage fingerpost signed for Torres Loan and Harelaw Cairn.
- Follow this path, muddy or very muddy at first, as it climbs past the edge of fields, going through three metal gates, passing under two sets of power lines and ascending Hare Law.
- At the top of the hill reach a gate at mile 20·6. Go through and turn left (signed for Cardenden) – unless you want to detour 100 m to visit Harelaw Cairn. The Way goes straight ahead on a path that becomes a track and then an unmade road (Torres Loan).
- Descend for over a mile (1·8 km) until the road forks. Bear right uphill and follow the track as it bends left. Descend to a gate at a junction with the tarmac access road.
- Turn right down the road for 450 m to reach the B921 near the edge of Cardenden. (Its railway station is just over a mile/1·7 km away.)
- With a FPW signboard on your left, turn left along the B921, soon passing Pilgrim Way Avenue.
- Walk along the pavement (on the left side of the road) for 1·9 miles (3 km) all the way to Kinglassie, following the B921 around a sharp right bend after 1·4 miles (2·2 km).
- From the bend, it's a further 0·7 mile (1·1 km) to and through the centre of Kinglassie to reach the Miners Welfare and Bowling Club on your left.
- On the far side of the bowling green, turn left through a gate and go up the signed path which climbs steeply up the edge of a grassy field.

Miners Welfare and Bowling Club, Kinglassie

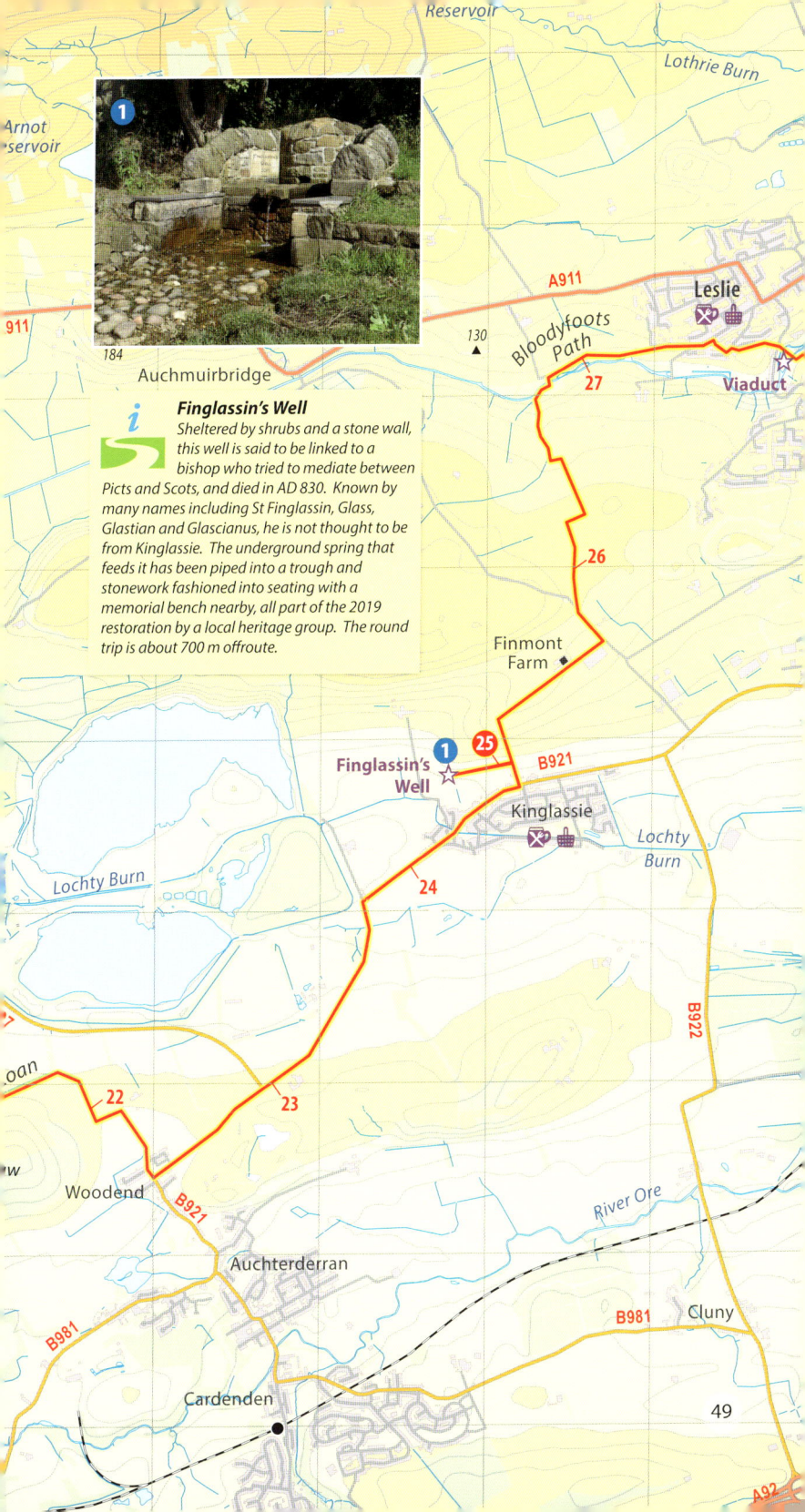

Finglassin's Well

Sheltered by shrubs and a stone wall, this well is said to be linked to a bishop who tried to mediate between Picts and Scots, and died in AD 830. Known by many names including St Finglassin, Glass, Glastian and Glascianus, he is not thought to be from Kinglassie. The underground spring that feeds it has been piped into a trough and stonework fashioned into seating with a memorial bench nearby, all part of the 2019 restoration by a local heritage group. The round trip is about 700 m offroute.

- After about 100 m, it's worth making the signed detour to the historic Finglassin's Well: see page 50. Afterwards retrace your steps to resume the climb.
- At the top of the hill the path is signed for Leslie and Glenorothes. It turns sharp right for 150 m before becoming a track and then a tarmac road through Finmont Farm. Follow it until it joins a public road at a T-junction. Turn left to walk briefly beside the road.
- After 220 m, just before the top of the hill, turn off the road right on a track that becomes a footpath. Follow it around a bend to the right, and where it forks, turn left to go downhill for 200 m.
- At the next path junction, go left again and after 60 m turn right to go downstream with the Den Burn on your left.
- Descend to the valley where it joins the River Leven. Walk beside it briefly before crossing over by a low stone bridge on the left at mile 26·8.
- Cross the small road and go through a gate with a fingerpost. Turn right to follow Bloodyfoots Path that runs parallel to the road, behind fencing. Follow it uphill for about 700 m to emerge on a lane at the back of houses in Leslie.
- Bear right and follow the track which after 100 m becomes a tarmac road (Walkerton Drive). Follow this road for another 300 m, where it merges with Prinlaws Road.
- To detour to Leslie, instead keep ahead past the Prinlaws (pub) towards cafés (Devine Cakes and Ela's) on the High Street. As we go to press, Leslie has no accommodation suited to walkers, but there are buses into Glenrothes for a wide choice. Otherwise, continue to the end of this section at the Leslie Viaduct.
- ⚠ After 90 m, look for the right turn down a narrow path which is easily missed: it's better to follow the pavement on the right side of the road, because on the left your access is hampered by railings.
- The path descends for 100 m to join Valley Drive, where you make a left-right dogleg into Valley Gardens. Follow the road to its end and continue after it becomes a path.
- Follow this path for a total of 300 m from Valley Drive to reach the Leslie Railway Viaduct over the River Leven at mile 27·8.

North-west from Bloodyfoots Path to West Lomond

Glenrothes

Before Glenrothes was developed, the main economic activities in the area were coal mining, farming and paper-making. The paper mills were established along the banks of the River Leven, which provided energy to power their operations. The name Glenrothes was created to join glen, meaning valley, with a link to the Earl of Rothes, whose family historically owned much of the land.

Glenrothes was planned in 1948 as Scotland's second post-war new town, and by 2011 it had a population of over 39,000. The original intention was to create a focus for industries, infrastructure and services to support the modern Rothes Colliery which started to produce coal in 1957.

However, as explained on page 22 the colliery closed prematurely and Glenrothes had to find new industries to support its economy. Electronic companies such as Rodime (which manufactured 3½ inch disc drives) were encouraged to come to Glenrothes as part of Scotland's 'Silicon Glen'. In 2017 the Glenrothes Energy Network was set up to deliver renewable biomass heat and power to local houses and offices.

In the mid-1970s, the town replaced Cupar as the headquarters of Fife Regional Council, making it the administrative centre of Fife. Glenrothes' place and importance in the history and development of Scotland has been enshrined in a panel of the Great Tapestry of Scotland, unveiled in 2013 in the Scottish Parliament. The Glenrothes panel portrays its public artworks and images from its mining heritage and current industries.

From Leslie, Stagecoach bus 39A will take you to Glenrothes bus station where you can connect with buses to Edinburgh, Cupar and St Andrews. There is also the route 31 which will take you back to Crosshill.

3·4 Leslie to Kennoway

Distance 9·7 miles 15·6 km
Terrain 75% on well-marked footpaths, with the rest on pavement
Grade mostly gentle gradients, with the last mile uphill to Kennoway
Food and drink Leslie, Markinch and Kennoway (cafés and shops in all three)
Summary pleasant and undemanding walking through Riverside and Balbirnie Parks to the historic town of Markinch, then beside the fields to Windygates and Kennoway

Leslie	2·5		2·6		4·6	Kennoway
27·8	4·0	Gilvenbank	4·2	Markinch	7·4	37·5

- Resume the Way by walking across the railway viaduct at mile 27·8. This 14-arched viaduct carried trains between Leslie and Markinch for over a century (1861-1967). It rises 80 feet above the valley floor and was designed by Thomas Bouch, infamous for the Tay Bridge disaster of 1879.

- On the viaduct's far side, look out for the sharp left turn onto a footpath leading into Riverside Park which links Leslie to parts of Glenrothes. Be alert for FPW signage on this stretch, as there are lots of colour-coded paths signed by FORP (Friends of Riverside Park) that you need to ignore.

- The path undulates through woodland for nearly a mile (1·5 km) with the river on your left. Emerge on a tarmac path and go down to a path junction with a large road bridge above (carrying the B969).

- If staying at the Holiday Inn Glenrothes, leave the route before it goes under the B969 bridge. Instead turn left to cross the river, go through the car park and continue up to the B969. The hotel is on the left near the A911/B969 roundabout.

- Go straight ahead to pass under the bridge and follow the footpath to another path junction where you keep straight on again and pass under a smaller bridge. Go straight ahead to pass under the bridge and follow the footpath to another path junction where you keep straight on again. Pass under another road bridge, this time the A911.

- After 400 m you emerge in the open park, with a children's play area and concrete hippopotamuses beside the river.

- After the playpark area, turn left to cross the River Leven by a metal footbridge. Follow the path as it rises among the trees.

The Leslie Viaduct, now used by walkers and cyclists

- After 200 m the path forks: bear left, and after a further 70 m at the next junction, go right.
- At the next junction, within 170 m turn left, and soon right to reach a public road. Go ahead through the pedestrian underpass under Cadham Road.
- You emerge on a quiet road, Iona Park. After 280 m bear slightly left where it merges with Pitcoudie Avenue, later passing the modern Christ's Kirk on your right.
- Soon after you enter Gilvenbank Sports Hub (home of Glenrothes Athletic FC), turn left along the signed tarmac path to go beside the pitches for 300 m.
- At a T-junction turn right, and after a further 200 m ignore a path that joins from the right. Keep on for 250 m to another T-junction where you ignore the wooden bridge to your left.
- Instead, turn right and after 180 m emerge from Gilvenbank at Huntsman's Road where you turn right along the pavement. After 90 m turn left into Kilmichael Road (unsigned).
- Walk along this road and after 400 m turn left towards Balfarg Steadings at a blue cycle sign. Go 200 m to its end and take the footpath which soon reaches the A92 dual carriageway.
- Turn left for 50 m to cross the A92 by the traffic lights. On the far side, descend to reach the footpath and turn right along it. Pass through the gap in the stone wall and descend for 100 m to Tofthill, the main road in Balbirnie Park.

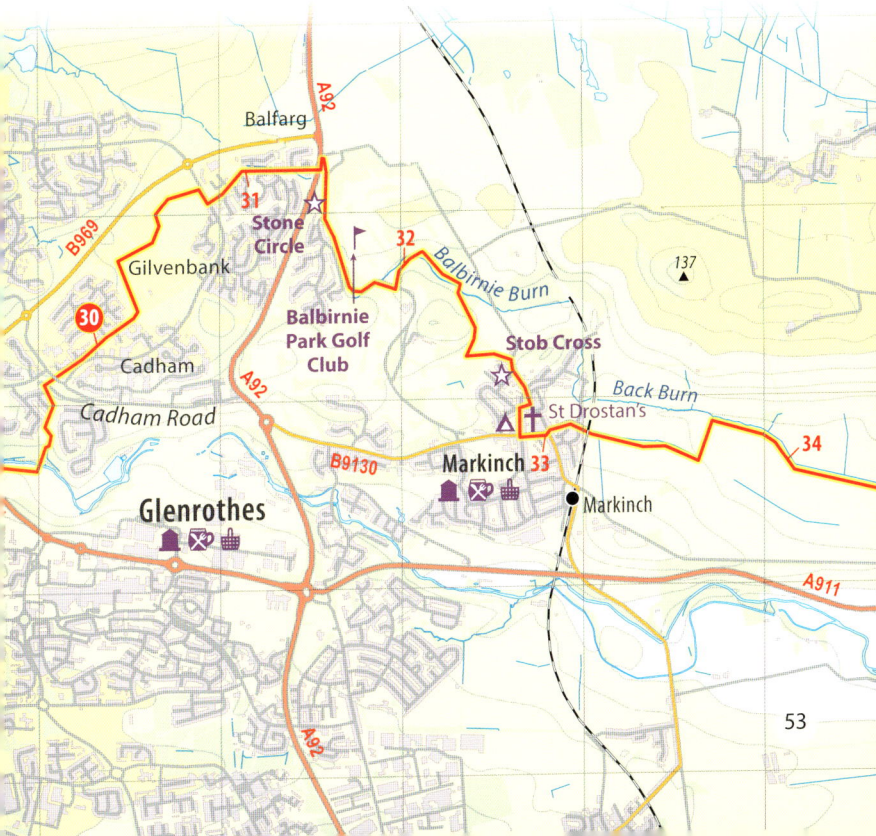

Balbirnie stone circle

- Turn right to follow the footpath beside the road for 250 m before crossing to turn left off the road, onto a path. Visit the Balbirnie stone circle with info board: it appears immediately on your right (mile 31·5).
- Continue straight ahead on this broad path for nearly 700 m through the trees until you come to the junction with the road for the golf course and its clubhouse. (If instead you went straight on you would reach Balbirnie House Hotel after 100 m or so.)
- Turn sharp left past the front of the clubhouse and go across the car park. Beyond it take the footpath into the trees.
- After 250 m cross Balbirnie Burn by a wooden footbridge and turn right to follow it downstream for 300 m. Turn right to recross the burn by footbridge, then ascend for 40 m to a signed T-junction.
- Turn left and follow the path for another 200 m. At the next junction, turn left down a narrow path.
- After 50 m it meets another path: turn left until you emerge from the park to meet Stob Cross Road.
- Cross over the road to turn right on its pavement, but immediately look back to the far side to see the historic Stob Cross on the mound above. There's a plaque about it on your side of the road.
- Follow the road into Markinch for 200 m to a junction with a FPW signboard and information about the Conservation Area on the right.

Stob Cross, the oldest monument in Markinch

Markinch

Markinch is a peaceful village with many historic buildings, and was the capital of Fife before Cupar. It is halfway between Dunfermline and St Andrews, and was probably a popular stop for medieval pilgrims who would have visited its church dedicated to St Drostan, a follower of St Columba.

The building that you see today has been remodelled several times, but has been in continuous use as a church since the early 12th century. Look for the distinctive cross at the entrance to its tower: see page 12. Its Norman tower is one of Scotland's finest, and its prominent location makes it a landmark from miles around. For visit details, see **www.markinchchurch.org.uk.**

St Drostan's parish church, with Norman tower

- With the signboard on your right, go ahead up Kirk Street to St Drostan's. Afterwards, descend the alley opposite (Gibbs Close) and turn left into Commercial Street.
- After 150 m reach a crossroads with the Laurel Bank Hotel on its far corner. You meet Balbirnie Street, Markinch's main road, and turn left along it.
- After 150 m reach another junction where the Way makes a left-right dogleg into Brunton Road. Before turning right into Brunton Road, look ahead up Glass Street for a fine view of St Drostan's and its commanding situation.

To detour to the railway station, at the end of Balbirnie Street turn right (instead of the left-right dogleg) and walk south on High Street for about 400 m. Markinch is on the main line between Edinburgh and Dundee.

North from the Way just beyond Markinch

- Follow Brunton Road to its end, and continue on the lane that passes under the railway bridge. Follow the path for 600 m before turning left for 220 m towards the Back Burn.

- The path now follows the edge of fields for the next 1·4 miles (2·3 km), always keeping the Back Burn on your left: don't be confused by a waymarker that seems to tempt you to cross the burn.

- At mile 35·1 leave the burn by turning sharp right at a path junction and 300 m later look for an inconspicuous waymarker that sends you left along another field-edge path. Look back for your last view of the tower of St Drostan's, clearly visible more than two miles away.

- After 600 m, at a track junction, go through the metal gate and follow the unmarked path (which widens to a track) for 800 m to the edge of Windygates. From this track you may see views of the double-summit of Largo Law ahead and slightly to your right.

Look back west for distant St Drostan's tower

- At Windygates, turn left into a minor road and maintain the same direction along Fa-Latch Road: don't get swept downhill and to the right into Main Street. After 650 m on this road, reach the main Kennoway Road (A916). Turn left uphill for 900 m to reach where the Way bears left into the old road (The Causeway).

- Follow The Causeway to rejoin the A916 after about 400 m. The Way continues by bearing left at mile 37·5. However, for Kennoway's shops, café and main bus stops, you need to backtrack about 100 m by turning sharp right (south) down the A916 to reach Bishop's Court.

  From Kennoway, Stagecoach buses 43 and 43A will take you to the main bus station at Glenrothes, where you can get buses in all directions.

3.5 Kennoway to Ceres

Distance 8.8 miles 14.2 km
Terrain about 90% on good paths and tracks
Grade a fairly sustained climb from Kennoway to the route's highest point (230 m/755 ft) on Clatto Hill
Food and drink Kennoway and Ceres (both with shops and cafés)
Summary a lovely rural walk through woodland and hill tracks, passing a fine reservoir; wide vistas, especially approaching Ceres

Kennoway —3.8— 6.1 —Clatto Hill— 5.0 —3.1— A916 —3.1— 1.9— Ceres
37.5   46.3

- Start in Kennoway from mile 37.5 and continue uphill on the pavement, passing St Kenneth's parish church with its fine war memorial. It names the dead from recent conflicts as well as both World Wars. The pavement soon runs along the right side of the road only, so you will have to cross over.

- About 800 m after the war memorial, look across the road for the sign announcing Bonnybank, with adjacent fingerpost and FPW waymarker post (mile 38.1). Cross the busy road with care here, and turn off left on the informal lane that runs between a field and houses at first, then narrows to a grassy path with ivy-clad trees.

War Memorial, St Kenneth's

Grassy path from Bonnybank

Clatto Reservoir

- The path climbs gently, and after 350 m crosses over a small road to Baintown. Keep straight along the path which descends to cross the Back Burn before climbing for 1·2 km, quite steeply at first.

- Approaching the top, pass through a gate (perhaps standing open) and go into some trees. At a fork, bear left and follow the path and go through a gate (signed Tilhill Forestry) to meet a bend in a broad forest road at mile 39·4: turn right.

- Follow this straight road for 1·2 km, then turn left uphill on a track through partly cleared woodland (Devon Wood) with young conifers set well back. After a further 1 km reach a T-junction with a minor road to Clatto Barns (mile 40·6).

- Turn sharp right up the road, and after 400 m, just beyond the cattle grid take the signed footpath on the left up through Edensmuir Forest.

- The track climbs to 230 m/755 ft near the top of Clatto Hill, and as you round a corner, a vista opens up ahead. Then descend through woodland, the track now rocky, before reaching a metal gate on the edge of Clatto Farm.

- Go through the gate and after 10 m turn right to walk for 200 m on a channel-fenced path; this bypasses the farm buildings on your left. Be alert for livestock in this area, which is prone to be muddy.

- At the end of the path (mile 42·4), go through the smaller of two gates and descend steeply into Clatto Den. After a further gate, follow the path around to the right to cross a small burn which then runs on your right.

- After 500 m you come to Clatto Reservoir and the path skirts its eastern end. The reservoir is a good place for seeing swans and various ducks. Near the end, if you turn sharply back left, a short path will take you to a viewing hide.

- At mile 42·7 you reach a car park area and follow the winding, potholed reservoir access road.

- Follow the access road for over 1 km to reach a junction with a minor road. Turn right uphill towards the hamlet of Muirhead.

- After 500 m of minor road, just after the left bend after Muirhead, leave the road by turning left after Stoorey Cottage to go through a gate into the field on your left at mile 43·4.

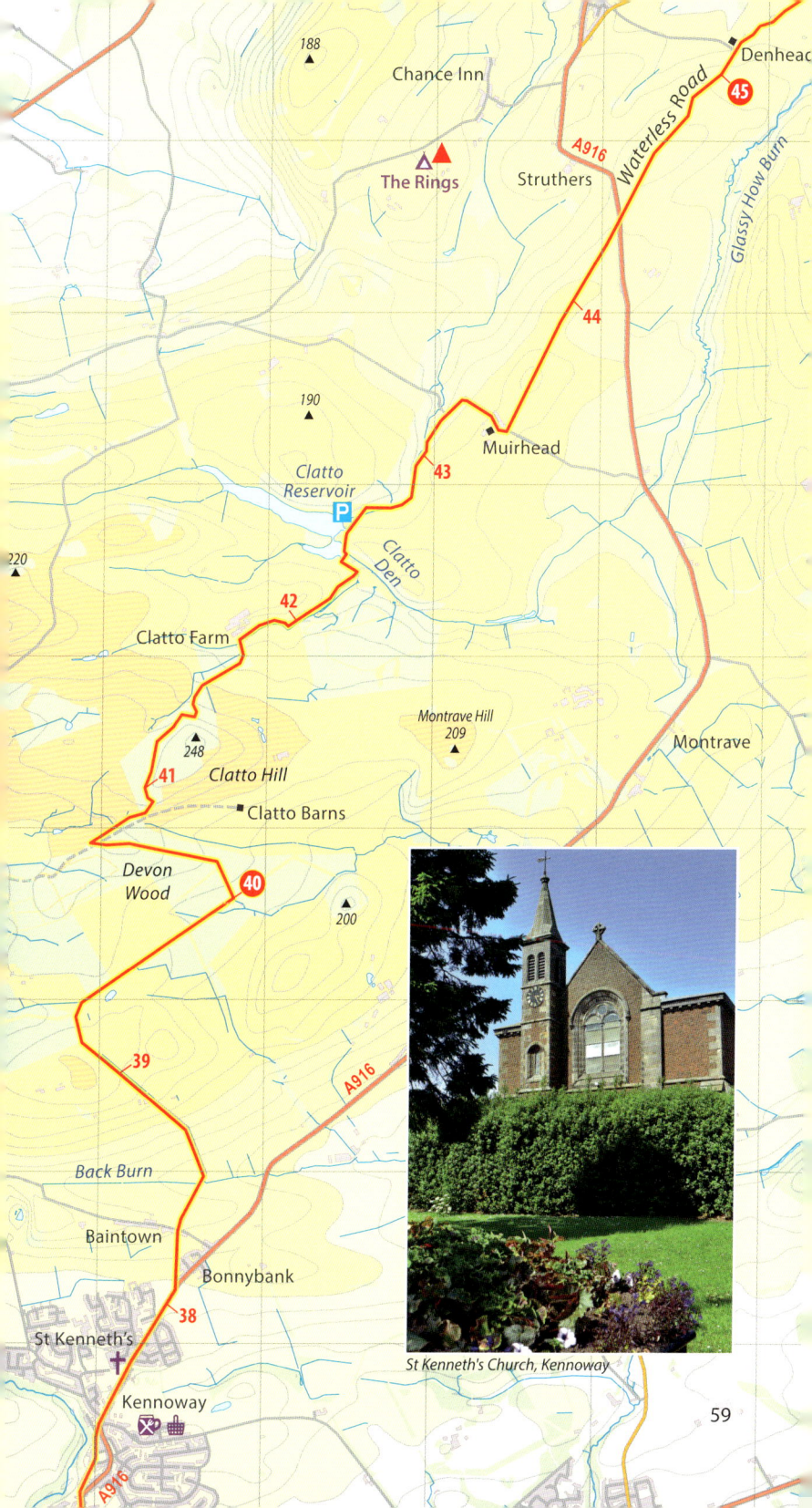

St Kenneth's Church, Kennoway

59

- Walk along this undulating field-edge path with a stone wall on your left and open views all around, passing through several gates before descending gently to some beech trees at the A916 main road.
- Cross straight over the busy road with care, and pick up the track opposite – the historic Waterless Road. It provides undulating walking which is pleasantly soft underfoot, though apt to be muddy in the wet.
- At Denhead (mile 45·2) the surface improves and a notice requests dogs to be on leads around the farm and its cottages. After 2 miles of pleasant Waterless Road the surface changes and you pass houses as you enter Ceres.
- At the bottom of the track, decide whether to stick to the Way, which bypasses the centre of Ceres to its south, or detour slightly for the parish church and other attractions of Ceres.
- To bypass Ceres and continue the Way, cross straight over the road into the main car park which has an FPW signboard. Aim for the fingerpost adjacent to the cobbled footbridge (Bishop's Bridge) to cross Ceres Burn.
- Alternatively, to visit the Coffee Shop and Fife Folk Museum, cross the car park diagonally and instead use the Folk Museum footbridge in the photo opposite. See the panel opposite for museum details.
- To visit the heart of Ceres, from the back of Fife Folk Museum head north up the High Street and cross the B939 (with bus stops) to reach shops, Ceres Inn and the excellent community-run Village Café, which is opposite the church: see page 62.
- Near the northern end of Main Street, you will find upmarket Meldrums Hotel and the Griselda Hill Pottery, which produces Wemyss Ware pottery.
- To resume the Way afterwards, return to the High Street and turn east into Castlegate: see page 63.

Bishop's Bridge across the Ceres Burn

Fife Folk Museum, Ceres

Fife Folk Museum

The Fife Folk Museum was founded in 1968 to celebrate the social, domestic and working lives of people in Fife. Its building combines weavers' cottages with a 1673 tolbooth and weighhouse with wall carving. It is open in season (from April 2024), admission free: www.fifefolkmuseum.org.
The dog-friendly Coffee Shop is open year-round, but out of season only from Wednesday to Sunday, 11.00 to 15.00: tel 01334 828 806.

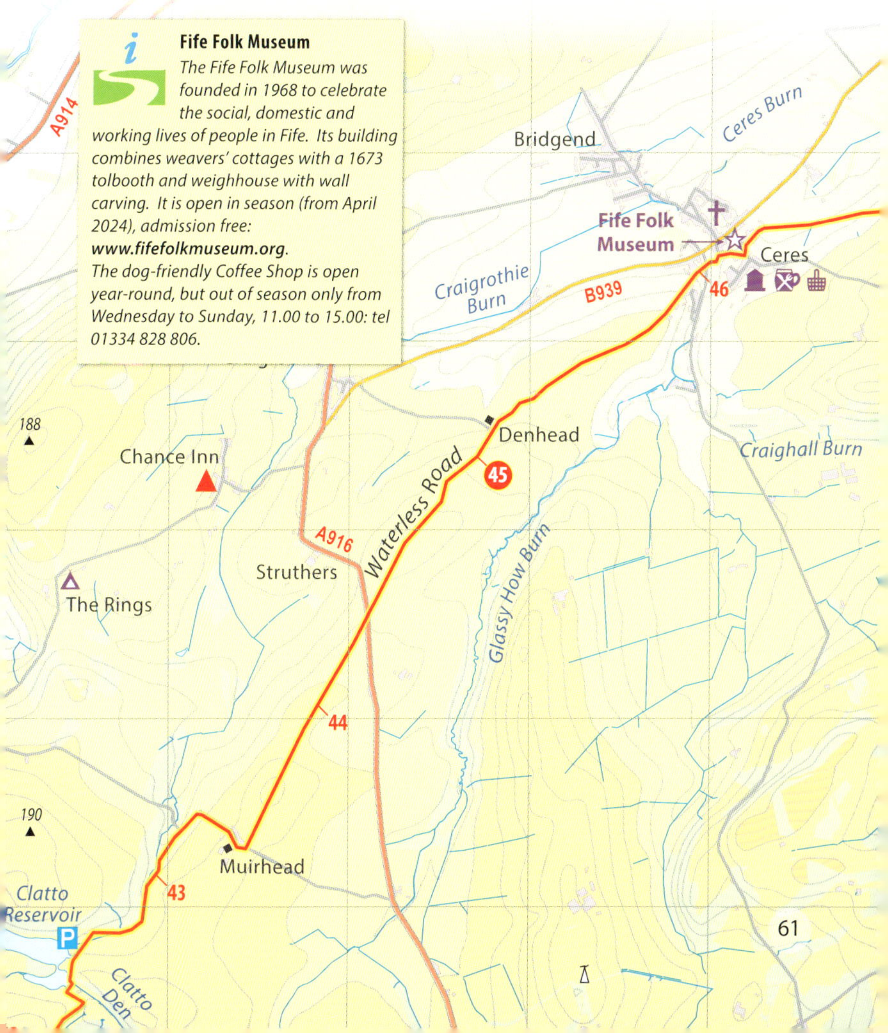

Ceres is an attractive village whose prosperity was founded on weaving and spinning linen. If you've 45 minutes to spare, follow the village heritage trail (under a mile) by visiting **bit.ly/RR-Ceres**. Otherwise start with the church, known as Ceres Kemback and Springfield since 2005, which stands on a site of worship and burial with a thousand-year history. The present church was built in 1806 to a design by Alexander Leslie, and its spire added in 1852. It contains a fine effigy of a knight and has box pews arranged in a way that allows most of the congregation to take communion seated at long tables. The Lindsay vault in the kirkyard may have been attached to a much earlier church built before 1274.

Ceres was long settled by the time of Bannockburn in 1314, where local men had fought alongside Robert the Bruce. After they returned, they held Highland Games on the village green, and this event has been held annually on the last Saturday in June ever since – the oldest Games in Scotland: see **www.ceresgames.co.uk**.

Ceres Kemback & Springfield Church

Near the crossroads with the B939 look for a Toby-jug style of statue in a niche in a wall. It depicts the Reverend Thomas Buchanan, the last church Provost in 1578. Originally carved in 1837 by John Howie, a local stonemason, the Provost moved to a different position in the village after local outrage was provoked by its sale to someone in Cupar.

From Ceres, Stagecoach bus 46 runs south-west back to Kennoway, or north to Cupar, with onward connections. Moffat and Williamson also run bus 64 which goes to Cupar and to St Andrews.

Bannockburn Memorial, Ceres

3·6 Ceres to St Andrews

| | | 64 | 65 | 67 |

Distance 9·7 miles 15·6 km
Terrain about 60% on good paths, 30% on quiet roads and 10% on the pavements of St Andrews
Grade short climb out of Ceres followed by a longer climb to Drumcarro (177 m/580 ft) with fine open views, then gradual descent into St Andrews
Food and drink Ceres (café and shops), Craigtoun Country Park (café), St Andrews (wide range)
Summary a pleasant, lofty walk through farmland before descending next to the Kinness Burn to reach St Andrews Cathedral

Ceres — 3·7 — 6·0 **Drumcarro** — 2·6 — 4·2 **Craigtoun Café** — 3·4 — 5·5 — **St Andrews**
46·3 .... 56·0

- From Ceres' main car park (mile 46·2), cross Ceres Burn by either bridge (see page 60) and head east along Castlegate. Follow its pavement for 150 m past houses on your right and a play park in the grass to your left.

- At the end of Castlegate bear left across Anstruther Road to the waymarked lamp-post in the triangular parking area fringed with grass. It leads you directly ahead to Schoolhill, where you turn right.

- Follow the pavement of Schoolhill for 120 m past the back of Ceres Primary School until the road ends. Go through the gate to your right on a narrow footpath between fields. The Way starts to climb gently, and after passing conifers on the left it enters a channel-fenced section leading to woodland.

- After about a mile, the path joins a broader farm track: very soon look for a sharp left turn (mile 47·4) that takes you down the side of the field.

- After 600 m, reach the bottom and turn sharp right along a rough farm road. Within 250 m this reaches the B940 road from Pitscottie (mile 47·8).

- Cross over the road and turn left over the road bridge. Immediately turn right along the private road that climbs to Kinninmonth Farm.

- Follow the road through the farmyard and cottages and continue on the track which climbs towards the summit of Kinninmonth Hill (169 m/555 ft).

- Before the summit, notice a stone seat on the left. Look behind you for a wonderful view back over Ceres to West Lomond, 15 miles away, with East Lomond to its left.

- Go on up over the cattle grid to a level section with views ahead left to St Andrews Bay and, on a clear day, the distant mountains of the north to your left. Keep straight on when you join a tarmac road to and through Ladeddie (mile 49·4). Follow the road's right-left bend through Drumcarro (mile 50·1).

West from the Kinninmonth track towards the Lomonds

West from the summit cairn towards the Lomonds

- The top of a mast ahead on your left soon reveals itself atop the rocky outcrop of Drumcarrow Craig (218 m/715 ft). The signed track for this detour leaves the road at mile 50·5. Don't be put off by the locked gate: squeeze past its post and after the next gate turn right along the access track for stunning views east-north-east over St Andrews.

- To reach the summit cairn, leave the access track to climb over broken bouldery ground, aiming for the mast until you see the cairn. On a clear day, your reward is an amazing panorama: high mountains to the north-west, the Lomonds to the west and Largo Law to the south-south-west.

Access track to Drumcarrow Craig

- About 100 m after the track sign, the road merges with a busier public road at mile 50·6: bear left.

- It climbs over a spur with views ahead of St Andrews Bay and the Eden estuary ahead. After 600 m, the road bends left but the Way forks right off it to follow a quieter lane.

- Descend through the hamlet of Denhead. Afterwards, join a long stone wall on your right, the boundary of the golf course. Before its end, at mile 51·6 turn right through a gap in the wall. It's well marked with a green fingerpost for Craigtoun Park and FPW signage.

- Through the gap, ignore the broken bits of fence ahead and immediately turn left on another path, keeping a wire fence to your right. After 120 m the path bears right at a low wall, which allows a view of St Andrews Bay across the field. Continue on the path through the trees with the Duke's golf course on your right for a further 700 m.

Boating lake at Craigtoun Country Park

- Near the end of the trees, the path seems to be heading down to a road, but instead bends right to a waymarker at a small tarmac circle. It points you up a short, steep tarmac slope to emerge at the 'Black Tee' of the Duke's golf course. Look for a view of St Andrews and its cathedral.
- Turn left down the path to reach a tarmac road at mile 52. Turn right and walk up the road for 500 m, passing the Duke's Clubhouse (bar and restaurant) on your left.
- A large sign announces the entrance to Craigtoun Country Park, and just beyond it, at a fingerpost, turn left through a metal gate, bearing slightly left at first.
- Follow the path through the park, and after passing ornamental columns framing an avenue of trees, turn right to pass a tall round tree feature and reach Craigtoun Café and a toilet block.
- Walk past (or visit) the café, then turn left to follow the path past a play park and picnic area, and exit the country park. Keep to a footpath down through the trees with Cairnsmill Burn on your right. At mile 53·4 cross a small road by metal gates.

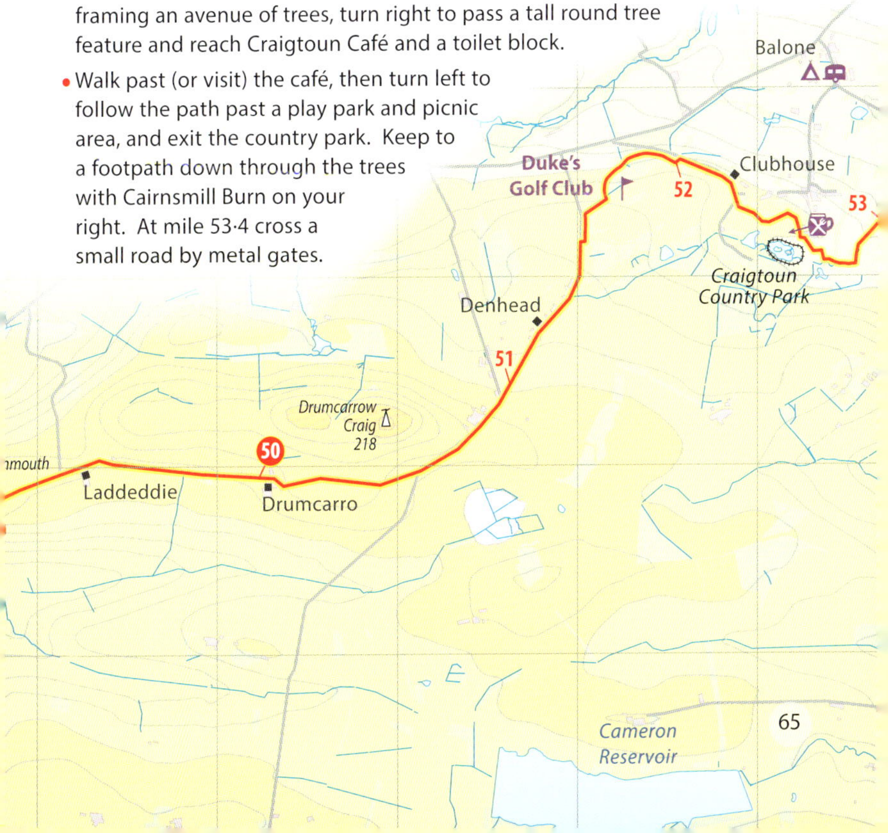

- Continue on the stony path with open views to north and east, high above Lumbo Den on your right. After about 500 m you start to pass houses at the edge of St Andrews and within 200 m you leave Lumbo Den to cross Bogward Road.
- Cross over the road and within 150 m pass the finely restored Bogward Dovecot to your left. Just after it, turn left on a path known as the Lade Braes.

Bogward Dovecot

- About 250 m after the Dovecot, reach a small mill pond, home to lots of ducks. The Cairnsmill Burn is about to join the Kinness Burn and you are about to switch to follow the Kinness Burn.
- Cross a stone arched bridge and turn immediately right to follow the Kinness Burn downstream, a 180° change of direction. Look back towards the mill pond and you'll see the large iron water-wheel at the side of the mill house.
- The Lade Braes continues as a well-marked path, meandering down through trees for a mile and into Cockshaugh Public Park with children's play park and football pitches.
- After the park, cross a minor road and bear right, still on the Lade Braes, to pass more houses. Within 300 m you reach the A915 (Melbourne Place) in St Andrews.

Lade Braes Walk passing Cockshaugh Park

- Cross over the A915 using the crossing to your left, and turn left uphill. Walk up for 80 m past a Shell garage to a small roundabout.
- Turn right and pass through the ancient arch (West Port Gate) into South Street. You are following in the footsteps of medieval pilgrims.

West Port

- Continue along South St for 350 m to reach the Holy Trinity Church on its left side. Beside this church, on its near side, is a pedestrian area with the final FPW signboard, explaining how the town's layout created a processional route for pilgrims. There's a blue Scottish Water topup post.
- Most readers will regard St Andrews Cathedral as their true destination. Walk a further 400 m along South St to reach the cathedral ruins. For its opening times and access, see page 68.
- Afterwards, for a place to sit still, contemplate or pray, we recommend you walk to nearby All Saints Episcopal Church. Walk north from the cathedral, and with your back to the war memorial, turn left along North Street. After 130 m, turn right along North Castle Street and enter the church courtyard on your left.

Congratulations on completing the Fife Pilgrim Way.

St Andrews

St Andrews is one of Scotland's most historic towns. It was once Scotland's ecclesiastical capital, home to bishops and archbishops, and frequented by monarchs. Scotland's first university was founded here in 1413, and it remains one of the most prestigious in Britain. It has about 12,000 students from over 145 nationalities, with nearly half its students coming from outside the UK.

The town's resident population is only about 17,000 but the town is recognised worldwide as the home of golf. The Royal and Ancient Golf Club is the international governing body of the sport, and golfers come from far and wide to play its famous Old Course. The town's popularity with visitors from North America makes for plenty of upmarket, expensive accommodation and restaurants. However the student population helps to support many budget options for eateries.

Swilken Bridge, The Old Course, St Andrews

Much of the old walled medieval city survives. The Way passes through its imposing West Port (gate), built in 1587 and refurbished in 1843. This leads to the ruined cathedral, on which the three ancient streets – North Street, Market Street and South Street – converge. The cathedral precinct is normally open to visitors daily year-round from 10.00 (with variable closing times), but check at **bit.ly/RR-sta**.

St Andrews has lots of other historic interest, for example the ruins of St Andrews Castle. The building dates from the 1400s, but was ruined during the Reformation. For more information on the town, visit the iCentre at 70 Market Street, tel 01334 472 021.

St Andrews Cathedral was once Scotland's largest and most magnificent church. Its construction began around 1160 and lasted for over 150 years: it was dedicated only in 1318. Over time, it was extensively damaged by storms and fire, but the attack at the start of the Reformation in 1559 proved terminal. The cathedral was abandoned in 1561 and its stones taken for use in other buildings – effectively reducing it to serving as the town's informal quarry.

The precinct contains the remains of two separate churches, with little surviving of a third church, St Mary on the Rock, outside the walls. The tallest structure within the site is St Rule's Tower, which rises to 100 ft and is in remarkable condition. St Rule's Church was begun in 1123, long before the cathedral, by Celtic monks and later extended by the Augustinian monks. Once it was realised that even the extended St Rule's would not suffice, work on the cathedral began.

When the tower is open, obtain a turnstile token to climb its 156 steps by a narrow spiral staircase. Your reward is a truly breathtaking view of the cathedral ruins, the town and its hinterland: see the photo below. The tower was due to reopen in spring 2024 but check *bit.ly/RR-sta*.

West from the tower over St Andrews Cathedral and Bay. Inset: St Rule's Tower

4 Reference

Organisations

The Way is managed, maintained and promoted by Fife Coast and Countryside Trust, an environmental and conservation charity based at The Harbourmaster's House, Dysart, Fife: *www.fifecoastandcountrysidetrust.co.uk*.

To find out more about the route and its heritage, visit the official website at *bit.ly/RR-FPW*. Scroll down for an interactive map showing points of interest, or click through to each of its sections: they match the seven sections in this book.

The Scottish Pilgrim Routes Forum is a network committed to developing pilgrimage routes across Scotland and to meeting the needs of pilgrim walkers and cyclists – people of all faiths and of none:
www.sprf.org.uk

NatureScot is the government agency that works to care for Scotland's nature. Its website is *www.nature.scot*

For details of the Scottish Outdoor Access Code: *www.outdooraccess-scotland.com.*

The latter site offers downloads of a pocket guide to the Code and (under *Practical guide for all*) leaflets for *Dog Owners* and for cyclists – *Off-road cycling: good practice advice.*

The Scottish Wildlife Trust cares for wildlife, campaigns on wildlife issues and develops practical conservation partnerships. It manages the Carlingnose Point nature reserve:
www.scottishwildlifetrust.org.uk.

Cyclists can seek advice from Cycling Scotland, CTC Scotland and Sustrans:
www.cyclingscotland.org
www.ctc.org.uk/scotland
www.sustrans.org.uk.

Historic Environment Scotland is the lead body that cares for Scotland's historic environment including many places that the Way visits: *www.historicenvironment.scot.* Here are shortcuts to entries for three key sites in Culross, Dunfermline and St Andrews:
bit.ly/RR-culr
bit.ly/RR-dunf
bit.ly/RR-sta

Web links and accommodation

Visit *www.rucsacs.com/books/fpw* for a list of useful websites, including listings, events and useful sources. In addition to VisitScotland (see below) *Welcome to Fife* lists accommodation in Fife:
www.welcometofife.com/accommodation

You can also try zooming in repeatedly on our online map (see below) as this sometimes reveals B&Bs that are close to the route but not listed in official directories.

VisitScotland is Scotland's overall tourist organisation. Its website *www.visitscotland.com* can be searched for accommodation, places of interest and travel. Its *iCentre* at St Andrews serves the Kingdom of Fife. 70 Market Street, St Andrews KY16 9NU, tel 01334 472 021, open all year.

Maps: printed and online

Footprint publishes a waterproof sheet map (*The Fife Pilgrim Way*, 2019) with mapping at the same scale as this guidebook, 1:40,000. In 2024 it cost £10.95, 978-1-916002-91-3. Beware: until there is a new edition, the map shows a number of B&Bs that no longer exist.

Ordnance Survey's Explorer series covers the route at larger scale (1:25,000) but you need three sheets: 367, 370 and 371. Note that (as of 2024) OS shows the route incorrectly in several places: near North Queensferry (miles 1·4 to 1·7) the route stays coastal, in Riverside Park (approaching mile 29) it never goes north of the River Leven, in Markinch the route passes St Drostan's (mile 32.8) and approaching Craigtoun Country Park, the Way enters the golf course at mile 51·6 and curves on its approach to mile 52. Always seek the latest edition of any map or guidebook.

Please visit our online route map at *www.rucsacs.com/books/fpw*
and zoom in for amazing detail in satellite view. As of 2024 this was the only source to show the route accurately and completely. Use it to search for accommodation and refreshments near the route.

Further reading

Bradley, Ian *The Fife Pilgrim Way* Birlinn, 2019 288 pp ISBN 978-1-78027-592-5
This book brings alive the communities, as well as the monks, miners and martyrs, whose footsteps you follow when you walk the Way. It is both authoritative and vividly well-written, with lots of illustrations,

anecdotes and four pages of bibliography. We readily acknowledge this as the single most important source for this book; for further reading suggestions, we recommend Bradley's bibliography.

Weather forecasts

The Met Office and BBC provide useful weather forecasts for 7 and 14 days ahead:
www.metoffice.gov.uk
www.bbc.co.uk/weather

Notes for novices

For those who lack experience of long-distance walking, there are notes on our website. Visit **www.rucsacs.com** and scroll down to click the yellow *Notes for Novices* button.

Transport

For travel from anywhere to anywhere, try **www.rome2rio.com**

For public transport throughout the UK, Traveline: **www.traveline.info**

For public transport within Scotland: **www.travelinescotland.com**

For bus travel in Fife, **www.stagecoachbus.com** is the main provider. See also **www.citylink.co.uk** and **uk.megabus.com**
and for buses in and around St Andrews **www.moffat-williamson.co.uk**

For rail travel and to buy tickets: **www.scotrail.co.uk** or **www.thetrainline.com**

Acknowledgements

We thank Fife Coast and Countryside Trust (FCCT) for its generous support for this guidebook and we warmly thank its staff for detailed comments on our drafts. We take responsibility for any defects that may remain.

Photo credits

Ian Clydesdale 29 (all three), 66 (lower two); Fife Council/Damian Shields front cover, 4-5, 7, 10 lr, 16l, 40u, 47u/back cover, 47l, 50, 54l, 58, 60, 61; FCCT 38, 49; Sandy Gerrard/geograph.org.uk 54u; William Hole, FRSA 15l; David Izatt 16u; Lynne Kirton 24u; Herbert Kratky /istockphoto.com 26u; Jacquetta Megarry 10 (five of six), 11, 12 (all six), 18 (all three), 24l, 25 (middle two) 26 (foot), 30 (both) 31, 32u, 33, 36 (both), 37 (both), 40l, 42, 44 (upper two), 46 (both), 48, 55, 56 (both), 57 (both), 63, 64 (both), 66u; Robert Struthers/geograph.org.uk 44l; topshotUK/istockphoto.com 25l; undiscoveredscotland.co.uk 52, 62l; University of St Andrews Library 14, 17, 20-21; VisitScotland/Kenny Lam 15u, 19u, 28l, 34, 36-7; VisitScotland/Damian Shields 65;

We thank *dreamstime.com* with the following photographers: Lightpoet title page; Konstantin32 p19/69u; Sasalan999 21, 22, 23, 45, 59, 62u; Whiskybottle 24l; Hakoar and Andreanita 25 upper two; Mille19 and Martin Pelanek 26 middle two; Orangeblossom 26l; Kellers 27u; Caglar Gungor 27m; BCritchley 27l; Pitsch22 28u; Jim Ryce 32l; Rudolf Tepfenhart 41, Julietphotography 68, Tw Van Urk 69l.

Churches along the Way

Below is a selection of churches that are on or near the Way. All have websites and you are advised to visit them and also to phone if you are keen to gain access. Some will arrange access on request, others may have to depart from their regular opening hours because of services, weddings and other events. A few combine two or more churches on different sites into a single congregation. Some may be willing to host pilgrims overnight if you contact them ahead of time: facilities are basic and this affects what you may need to bring.

Location	Church	Website	Page
Cairneyhill	Cairneyhill Parish Church	www.cairneyhillchurch.org.uk	31
Dunfermline	Dunfermline Abbey	www.dunfermlineabbey.com/wwp	33,40
Dunfermline	St Margaret's Memorial Church	www.stmargaretsdunfermline.co.uk	42
Kelty	Kelty Church/Church at the Cross	www.keltychurch.co.uk	43
Kinglassie	Kinglassie Parish Church	www.auchterderrankinglassieparishchurch.org	49
Glenrothes	Christ's Kirk	www.christskirk.uk	53
Markinch	St Drostan's/Markinch and Thornton Parish Church	www.markinchchurch.org.uk	55
Kennoway	St Kenneth's Parish Church	www.stkenneths.org.uk	57,59
Ceres	Kemback & Springfield Church	www.ckschurch.org	62
St Andrews	Holy Trinity Church	www.holyt.co.uk	18,67,68
St Andrews	All Saints Episcopal Church	www.allsaints-standrews.org.uk	67,68

Index

A
Abbot House 42, 43
accommodation 6, 8, 50, 70

B
Balbirnie Park, stone circle 53, 54
bike shops 6
bloody cranesbill 24
Bloodyfoots Path 50
butterflies, common blue 24

C
Cairneyhill 8, 31
Carnegie, Andrew 32, 39
Ceres 6, 8, 20, 60-62, 63
Clatto Hill 10, 11, 58
Clatto Reservoir 27, 58
Crosshill 6, 8, 46, 47, 48
Culross 5, 6, 8, 9, 15, 28, 29, 70
Cupar 51, 55, 62
cycling 6, 70

D
distances and time needed 6, 7
dogs 11, 60, 70
Dunfermline 5, 6, 8, 9, 14, 15, 16-17, 32-3, 39-40, 41, 42,

E
eider duck 25

F
facilities along the route 8
field vole 26
Fife Coast and Countryside Trust 70, 71
Fife Coastal Path 13, 29, 30, 36
Fife, Kingdom of 5, 14,
Forth bridges 35, 39

G
gannet 25
Glenrothes 6, 8, 22, 51, 52,
golf, golf courses 54, 64, 65, 68
gradients 10-11

H
habitats and wildlife 24-27
hare, brown 26

K
Kelty, Keltybridge 8, 21, 22, 23, 45
Kennoway 6, 8, 56, 57
kingfisher 27
Kinglassie 8, 22, 48, 49
Kingseat 44
Knox, John 18

L
Leslie 6, 8, 50, 52
livestock 11
Lindsay pit, colliery 20-21, 22

Loch Fitty 27, 44
Lochore Meadows 4-5, 8, 22, 23, 46, 47
Lomonds, West and East 50, 63, 64

M
Malcolm III (Malcolm Canmore), King 15, 32
maps 70
Markinch 8, 54, 55, 56
Margaret, Queen (later Saint) 5, 14, 15-16, 17, 34, 41
miners and mining 20-23

N
North Queensferry 5, 6, 9, 15, 34, 36
Notes for novices 7, 71

O
oystercatcher 25

P
packing checklist 13
pilgrims, pilgrimage 5-7, 12,14-19, 55, 66, 67, 70
Protestantism 14, 18, 19
public transport 6, 7, 8, 9, 33, 40, 71

R
Reformation 15, 16, 18, 19, 43, 68, 69
Robert the Bruce, King 41, 62
Rosyth 8, 9, 38

S
St Andrew 14, 17, 18
St Andrews 4, 5, 6, 7, 8, 9, 12, 14, 16, 17-19, 64, 66-7, 68-9, 70, 71
St Drostan 55
St Margaret 5, 14, 15-16, 17, 34, 41
St Mungo (Kentigern) 5, 15, 30
St Rule's Church, Tower 69
St Serf 5, 15
Scottish Outdoor Access Code 6, 11, 70
Scottish Pilgrim Routes Forum 14, 70
sea buckthorn 25
Stob Cross 54

T
tern, common 24, 25
terrain 10
transport and travel 6, 7, 8, 9, 33, 40, 71

V
Valleyfield 21, 25, 30

W
waymarking 12-13
weather 6, 78
wren 27

Y
yellowhammer 27